Shiba Inu

Shiba Inu Dog Complete Owners Manual

Shiba Inu Basics, Choosing and Owning, Breeding, Care, Feeding, Grooming, Showing and Training All Included!

By: Lolly Brown

Copyrights and Trademarks

All rights reserved. No part of this book may be reproduced or transformed in any form or by any means, graphic, electronic, or mechanical, including photocopying, recording, taping, or by any information storage retrieval system, without the written permission of the author.

This publication is Copyright ©2021 NRB Publishing, an imprint of Pack & Post Plus, LLC. Nevada. All products, graphics, publications, software and services mentioned and recommended in this publication are protected by trademarks. In such instance, all trademarks & copyright belong to the respective owners. For information consult www.NRBpublishing.com

Disclaimer and Legal Notice

This product is not legal, medical, or accounting advice and should not be interpreted in that manner. You need to do your own due-diligence to determine if the content of this product is right for you. While every attempt has been made to verify the information shared in this publication, neither the author, neither publisher, nor the affiliates assume any responsibility for errors, omissions or contrary interpretation of the subject matter herein. Any perceived slights to any specific person(s) or organization(s) are purely unintentional.

We have no control over the nature, content and availability of the web sites listed in this book. The inclusion of any web site links does not necessarily imply a recommendation or endorse the views expressed within them. We take no responsibility for, and will not be liable for, the websites being temporarily unavailable or being removed from the internet.

The accuracy and completeness of information provided herein and opinions stated herein are not guaranteed or warranted to produce any particular results, and the advice and strategies, contained herein may not be suitable for every individual. Neither the author nor the publisher shall be liable for any loss incurred as a consequence of the use and application, directly or indirectly, of any information presented in this work. This publication is designed to provide information in regard to the subject matter covered.

Neither the author nor the publisher assume any responsibility for any errors or omissions, nor do they represent or warrant that the ideas, information, actions, plans, suggestions contained in this book is in all cases accurate. It is the reader's responsibility to find advice before putting anything written in this book into practice. The information in this book is not intended to serve as legal, medical, or accounting advice.

Foreword

This instructional guide will discuss all of the things that you need to know in order to get started as an owner of a Shiba Inu. Bringing home a new addition for the first time can be a really exciting endeavor. The whole family may have spent time picking out the puppy that they wanted to bring home, and now they are excited to bond with her and to make some lasting memories.

This guidebook is going to walk you through the steps that you need to follow in order to raise your Shiba Inu well, get your puppy trained and ready to behave.

Included inside this book's first section is about the origin and bio of a Shiba Inu. It contains the general information and the characteristics of this specific dog breed.

The Second section is about choosing a Shiba Inu. It tackles about where and how to acquire a Shiba Inu and how to select a healthy Shiba Inu puppy.

The next section will talk about the things that you need and have to do as a Shiba Inu owner.

The fourth section focuses on how you can cater your dog's nutritional needs.

The next section delves into basic care and regular grooming needs for your Shiba Inu.

The sixth section is about raising and training your Shiba Inu. It educates dog owners about the importance of training and activities for your dog. It additionally contains a puppy's training outline and guidance in shaping behaviors, training, and problem solving.

Th seventh section focuses on the common health issues and how to deal with them and respond into emergencies.

Chapter eight is about preparing your Shiba Inu for a dog show.

For the last section, it will talk about the breeding process for your Shiba Inu.

By obtaining this training guide, you will be on your way to securing the necessary tools and knowledge to assure your success as a Shiba Inu dog owner and trainer.

Table of Contents

Introduction 1
Chapter One: Shiba Inu Facts and Descriptions 3
    General Information 3
    Brief History 4
    Dog Breed Characteristics 4
Chapter Two: Choosing and Acquiring a Shiba Inu 7
    Choosing Your Puppy 8
    Where to Get a Shiba Inu 10
    Identifying Good Breeders 15
        Who is a Good Breeder? 16
        Questions to Ask a Shiba Inu Breeder 20
        Questions from a Shiba Inu Breeder 23
Chapter Three: Preparing for Your Shiba Inu 27
    Supplies and Equipment Needed 27
    Dog-proofing Your Home 34
Chapter Four: Feeding Your Shiba Inu 37
    How Much Food Does Your Shiba Inu Need? 38
    Essential Nutrients Needed by the Shiba Inu 39
        Protein 39
        Healthy Fats 40
        Carbohydrates 41

Fiber 41

Other Essential Vitamins and Minerals 42

What the Shiba Inu Diet Should Not Contain? 42

Basics of Feeding the Shiba Inu 44

Is it Safe to Feed a Shiba Inu Human Food? 47

Chapter Five: Grooming Your Shiba Inu 51

Skin and Coat 51

Brushing and Combing 53

Bathing 55

Teeth 57

Nails 59

Eyes and Ears 61

Chapter Six: Training and Behavior Modification 63

Housebreaking Your Puppy 63

What to Expect 64

How to Housebreak Your Puppy 65

Crate Training 66

Umbilical Training 68

Using a Bell at the Door 69

Teaching Your Puppy to Follow Commands 69

Basic Commands 74

Sit 74

- Stay 75
- Down 76
- Come 77
- Off 78
- Drop 79
- Leave 80
- Gently 80
- Speak 81
- Putting the Basics Together 81

Separation Anxiety 82
- Causes and Signs Of Separation Anxiety 83
- What To Watch Out For 86
- Why Punishment Won't Work 87
- Preparation and Socialization 89
- How To Leave And Return 93
- Leaving When Using A Crate 95
- Some Other Useful Tips 96
- The 10 Steps To Help Separation Anxiety 97

Common Behavior Problems 98
- Jumping up on Other People 99
- Destructive Chewing 101
- Pulling on the Leash 103

The Puppy Doesn't Want to Walk on the Leash 105

Too Much Roughhousing with the Puppy 106

Fearfulness 108

The Escape Artist 109

Too Much Whining and Barking 111

Being on the Furniture 114

Digging 115

Chapter Seven: Vet Care for Your Shiba Inu 119

Signs of Illness 120

Bad Breath 120

Drooling 120

Loss of Appetite 121

Excessive Thirst 121

Changes in Urination 121

Skin Problems 122

Lethargy 122

Common Diseases/Illnesses 122

Finding a Good Vet 128

Vaccinations 129

Educate Yourself About Common Canine Diseases and Viruses 131

Be Aware That Allergies Can Adversely Affect Your Dog's Health 131

Spaying and Neutering 132

Pet Health Insurance 133

Chapter Eight: Showing Your Shiba Inu 135

Showing Shiba Inu Dogs.. 136

What to Know Before You Show 137

Preparing Your Dog for Show.. 139

Chapter Nine: Breeding Your Shiba Inu............................... 141

Choosing Dogs To Breed 142

    Health 143

    Clearances 143

    Registration 143

    Temperament.. 144

    Bloodlines... 144

    Age 144

    Physical Traits.. 145

Breeding your Shiba Inu 146

    The Heat 147

Natural or Artificial? 148

When to Breed 149

The Act of Breeding 151

Is She Pregnant? 153
Whelping your Pups.. 155
Whelping Supplies... 155
    Before Labor... 158
    First Stage Labor.. 158
    Second Stage of Labor 159
    Third Stage of Labor 160
Raising Puppies.. 162
Puppy Development.. 168
Conclusion 173
Glossary of Terms 175
Index 181
Photo Credits 189
References 193

Introduction

The Shiba Inu is well-known for its devotion, willingness to please and intelligence. No wonder its popularity is always sky high. A Shiba Inu makes a great family pet and will spice up any home environment. However, there is a lot you need to know before going out and getting a Shiba Inu.

You could be planning to adopt a Shiba Inu puppy or maybe you already have one and want to educate yourself more about this dog breed. This means you should research the most relevant material there is on how to choose, raise, care for and train a Shiba Inu.

This comprehensive guide will teach you all you need to know about and to care for Shiba Inus, starting from the history of this breed all the way to the hereditary Shiba Inu diseases that you will want to be aware of and the breeding process. You will also learn how to choose the right breeder and what to do when picking your puppy.

Proper care is of the utmost importance, and you will learn how to properly feed, groom, and train your puppy.

There is so much to learn when adopting a Shiba Inu. I want to make sure you get it right although there will always be surprises; hopefully mostly pleasant. If you utilize the information in this book, you will end up with a happy Shiba

Introduction

Inu that will serve you for many years to come. You will also be a happy dog owner and healthier as a result.

Are you ready to learn more about Shiba Inus?

Let's get started!

Chapter One: Shiba Inu Facts and Descriptions

General Information

Dog Name: Shiba Inu

Dog Breed Group: Companion dogs

Size Category: Small dog breeds

Height: Ranges from one foot, one inch to one foot, five inches (measured from the shoulder).

Weight: Ranges from 17 to 23 pounds.

Chapter One: Shiba Inu Facts and Descriptions

Lifespan: Ranges from 12 to 16 years.

Brief History

The Shiba Inu is the smallest of the six distinct breeds of dog that are native to Japan. It can be seen in ancient drawings dating back to the third century, in which it is depicted chasing small animals. This breed is known for being quick and nimble, qualities that made them perfect hunting dogs during Japan's period of military rule (Kamakura Shogunate). Nowadays, these small dogs are most often found in Japan and the USA, where they are popular companion dogs.

Dog Breed Characteristics

A. Protection Ability

Their natural distrust of strangers makes the Shiba Inu a passable watch dog. Whilst they will bark to alert their owners of unfamiliar people, they generally will not attack or even approach strangers.

Score: 4/10

B. Ease of Training

Despite their intelligence, the Shiba Inu is notoriously difficult to train. They are tremendously independent, and so whilst they may understand what their owner is asking of them, they will not always want to comply. The best approach to training the Shiba Inu is make them believe the obedience is their idea. Fortunately, this breed is naturally clean and very receptive to housebreaking.

Score: 5/10

C. Playfulness

The Shiba Inu is a moderately energetic breed which forms tight attachments to their owners and children. This means that whilst they are generally very playful with people they know, they can be a little aloof with strangers. This breed has described as "cat-like" in its behaviors; it enjoys being lavished in attention, but it's also perfectly content with lounging around the house alone.

Score: 6/10

D. Exercise needs

Whilst it's true that Shiba Inus are not the most energetic of breeds, they do need daily exercise in order to stave off boredom and aggression. They typically are happiest with one daily walk, during which they must stay on the lease, due to their prey instinct and their potential for dog-aggression.

Score: 5/10

E. Adaptability

The Shiba Inu is very adaptable to changes in their environment, and they are suited to apartment living. They can be left alone during the day, and they behave well around children (provided that they are treated respectfully).

Score: 8/10

Chapter One: Shiba Inu Facts and Descriptions

Chapter Two: Choosing and Acquiring a Shiba Inu

In this chapter, you will learn how to find a good Shiba Inu puppy. There are several very important considerations that you must make as you look at a litter of pups. On top of that, you must also consider the source of your Shiba Inu.

- Do you intend to buy from a breeder or adopt from a shelter?
- How about a rescue organization?

We will look at some of the potential sources of Shiba Inu puppies toward the end of this chapter.

Let's start by learning how to choose your Shiba Inu puppy.

Chapter Two: Choosing and Acquiring a Shiba Inu

Choosing Your Puppy

It can be a very exciting experience looking at a litter of cute and cuddly Shiba Inu pups. They all look so adorable and you almost wish you could take them all home with you. However, this is not the time to allow your emotions to get the best of you. There are certain factors you must consider before taking that plunge.

1. *Always purchase your puppies from a responsible breeder* - We usually refer to them as "ethical breeders" or "hobby breeders." These are breeders who are officially recognized by the national association of that particular country. If you live in the UK or U.S., make sure the breeder is registered with the UKC or AKC respectively.

    a. Working with an ethical breeder is important because they will help you pick the right puppy. They will share with you the health records of the puppy you want and make sure that you get a dog that has been properly socialized.

    b. *Socialization* involves teaching a dog how to relate to people and other animals so that they are neither overly aggressive nor too shy. This is absolutely critical to raising a healthy and happy dog.

Chapter Two: Choosing and Acquiring a Shiba Inu

A responsible breeder will also make sure that they remove the puppy's dew claw and vaccinate the entire litter before they reach six weeks of age. You should also note that a responsible breeder will never sell a puppy under the age of seven weeks.

2. **_Determine your personal preferences_** – What kind of Shiba Inu would you like to have? This is where you have to look at things like temperament, coat color, behavior, and etc. If you want a calm dog that won't be too hyperactive, look for a puppy that behaves that way. If you lead an active lifestyle, then go for a puppy that is more exuberant.

3. **_Look at the behavior of every puppy in the litter_** - When you meet the litter for the first time, you may notice that different puppies behave differently, even though they have the same set of parents.

    a. For example, one puppy in the litter may be too shy while the others appear friendly. This may be a cause for concern because the litter shares the same genes.

    b. If you are looking for a social dog, then you may have to pick from a different litter. The same advice applies to puppies that appear to be extremely hyperactive.

4. **_View the parents_** – It is always a good idea to view both parents, if possible. A responsible breeder should have at least one of the parents on site. This

Chapter Two: Choosing and Acquiring a Shiba Inu

will help you get a good look at what your puppy will look like in the future.

These are just some of the factors that will help you make the ideal choice when buying a Shiba Inu puppy. If you are aware of what to look out for, you will end up with a well-bred dog that is the perfect companion for your family.

Where to Get a Shiba Inu

Making the decision of where to get your Shiba Inu puppy can be a tough one. You are walking home one day, you see a pet store, and you decide to check out what they have. You fall in love with a terribly cute, chocolate-colored Shiba Inu puppy. You start to imagine what it would feel like to own the dog.

When you get home, your friend calls and tells you that her Shiba Inu bitch has just given birth to a litter of pups. She asks you to think about adopting one or two. Later on, you switch on the TV and see a program about dogs that have been rescued by a local shelter. You begin to feel philanthropic and contemplate saving an abandoned Shiba Inu puppy.

You are split on the choices about where to get the puppy of your dreams. You can go to the pet store, adopt one from your friend's litter, or rescue an abandoned pup. Then you remember something you read in a Shiba Inu eBook that recommended you only buy puppies from a responsible breeder. Darn! Now what?

Chapter Two: Choosing and Acquiring a Shiba Inu

When it comes to finding a Shiba Inu puppy, there are so many options that you may face. However, each choice has its pros and cons. Some options, however, are downright unethical and shouldn't even be contemplated.

Let's run through these options so that you know exactly what to do when it's time to make a choice.

Option 1: The Pet Store

There are many people who consider this to be a good option. Some dog owners will testify that they bought their Shiba Inu puppy from a pet store and everything went okay. However, out of the four options presented above, this is considered to be the worst, and here's why.

- The majority of the dogs you see in pet stores *have been sourced from "puppy mills."* In case you don't know what this means, a puppy mill is a farm where puppies are bred in terrible conditions. They are put in tiny cages where they barely get any exercise and cannot even socialize with other dogs or humans. Many local cities have now banned this practice.

- The people who run these mills (commercial and backyard breeders) aren't interested in the welfare of the dogs. All they care about is selling them off as quickly as possible to make room for the next batch. They then sell off these puppies to pet stores for people to buy. This is why some countries have even banned pet stores from selling puppies.

Chapter Two: Choosing and Acquiring a Shiba Inu

According to a study conducted by the American Veterinary Medical Association, dogs that are bought in pet stores have a higher chance of developing health problems and generally require more expensive treatment throughout their life. These dogs tend to endure a lot of suffering and this is why most of them have a higher likelihood of developing behavioral and psychological problems.

There are many people out there who will doubt this information. They will tell you that it's okay to buy from a pet store. However, if we are going to put an end to the inhumane conditions that these puppies live through in puppy mills, we have to stop supporting this practice. There are other better sources.

Option 2: Gift from a Friend

Though your friend may be a really good person at heart and isn't really an unethical breeder, is she a professional breeder? In other words, was her litter of pups bred with the care and consideration that a responsible breeder provides? It's highly unlikely although not always the case. In fact, that litter of pups was probably a welcome surprise to her.

There are certain risks that come with allowing your dog to breed. The father may not have been screened to determine whether he will produce healthy Shiba Inu puppies. Your friend may have bred her dogs without considering the puppies' appearance, health, or temperament. She probably didn't even factor in genetic or behavioral diseases.

Chapter Two: Choosing and Acquiring a Shiba Inu

You are probably thinking of how much money you will save by grabbing the free gift. Maybe you don't want to see the puppies end up in a rescue organization. However, it's important to understand that there may be some costly health or behavior surprises later on when your puppy grows up. You may find yourself overwhelmed by veterinary expenses and behavioral problems.

The puppy may end up being an awesome pet, but you need to know that the risks can be avoided. Accepting to adopt a puppy from your friend is an option, but it really isn't the best one of all but if you are firmly set on it, then please go ahead.

Option 3: The Animal Shelter/Rescue Center

This is a good option for anyone looking to adopt a Shiba Inu in need of a home. There are millions of dogs that find themselves without a home every year, and most of them end up in animal and rescue homes.

Shiba Inus make up a huge percentage of these dogs because they are one of the most popular breeds in almost every English-speaking country.

If they are unable to find a good home or the shelter runs out of funds or space, these poor creatures are usually put down. Therefore, adopting a Shiba Inu from an animal shelter or rescue center is a great thing to do. The dog that is usually housetrained won't chew on your belongings and will already be screened and tested for any health issues.

However, there are still a few risks. Some of these dogs may have been abandoned because they developed behavioral or health problems. Some may be psychologically scarred due to the neglect and abuse they suffered. The dog may not show any of the effects at first glance, but under certain situations, you may see an unusual level of aggression.

On the other hand, shelter dogs can make amazing pets if you love them and teach them how to cope in their new environment. Plus, you get to save a dog that would otherwise have been euthanized. This is indeed a better option than a pet store or getting a dog from a friend.

Option 4: The Professional Breeder

This is the recommended source for anyone who wants to own a Shiba Inu. You will get a healthy and quality dog from a person who actually cares about the welfare of their animals.

Responsible breeders do not breed dogs for profit but for their love of dogs and the specific breed. While it's true that they do sell their dogs, the amount of money a responsible breeder makes is usually minimal. It costs a lot of money to set up a registered breeding program where dogs are fed the best food, given great veterinary care, undergo regular tests, and are bred to exhibit specific traits.

Unlike backyard breeders, the ultimate goal of a responsible breeder isn't to make huge profits. It is to enhance the gene pool and ensure that every Shiba Inu they produce

Chapter Two: Choosing and Acquiring a Shiba Inu

is purebred and of the highest pedigree. This is why they are also referred to as "hobby breeders."

This is the best option for you, and to find out more about responsible breeders, read the next section.

Here are three key points to remember:

1. When choosing a puppy, you need to consider certain factors. These include the source of the puppy, its behavior, its parents, and your personal preferences.

2. There are many options when looking to buy or adopt a Shiba Inu puppy. Some are not recommended at all, for example, pet shops. Others, such as adopting a friend's puppies, are good but carry inherent risks. Cheap is not always best.

3. Adopting a Shiba Inu puppy or and adult dog from a shelter/rescue center is a great idea. You may be saving a dog from being put down. However, the best option is always to buy from a responsible breeder.

Identifying Good Breeders

When it comes to finding a Shiba Inu puppy, there are responsible breeders and then there are others that are not so responsible. In this chapter, you will learn what to expect

Chapter Two: Choosing and Acquiring a Shiba Inu

from a breeder so that you are well placed to separate the good from the bad.

Some people think that the most important thing is the appearance or health of the puppy. However, if you buy from an unethical breeder, you are practically guaranteed to end up with a puppy with poor health and unsound temperament. ***Never let appearances fool you.*** You need to learn how to identify a good breeder by assessing specific traits and factors.

Who is a Good Breeder?

A good breeder, in this case, refers to an ethical and responsible person who breeds dogs. However, two things that characterize a good Shiba Inu breeder are:

- their intense love for the breed
- and their active engagement in dog competitions, for example, dog shows and field trials.

A person doesn't just wake up one day and become a good breeder simply because their dog is in heat and they want to have puppies. Good breeders are never driven by profits either. There's barely any money to be made from breeding anyway.

A good breeder is dedicated and willing to spend the time, money, and effort to produce purebreds that will add value to people's lives. A good Shiba Inu breeder must be concerned about the overall welfare of all Shiba Inus. They care about the mother's health so that the puppies can start their lives in the best way possible.

Chapter Two: Choosing and Acquiring a Shiba Inu

Let's look at four key traits that will help you identify a good breeder.

Selective Matching of Sire and Dam

A good breeder doesn't take any random sire (male) and dam (female) and mate them. *They select the sire and dam carefully with a specific purpose in mind.* For example, a good breeder will pick a sire and dam specifically to produce puppies that will excel in field trials and competitions. They will choose a sire and dam for puppies that can perform well in the show ring. They can also breed specifically for obedience.

Each of the disciplines mentioned above has different requirements. A good breeder knows that the judges will be looking for certain qualities depending on the discipline.

On the other hand, a breeder can also breed dogs that simply make good house pets. A good breeder is focused on assessing the strengths and weaknesses of the sire and dam so that their puppies can achieve the desired goal and purpose.

This is much different from the way an unethical breeder operates. An unethical breeder doesn't even care about selecting for a purpose. They will use any dog they can find, as long as they are of the same breed. They don't consider whether the parents are compatible and how the puppies will turn out.

Chapter Two: Choosing and Acquiring a Shiba Inu

Care About Puppy Living Conditions

If you contact a breeder and they tell you that they will bring you the Shiba Inu puppy, or ask you to meet them in some random place, you are likely dealing with an unethical breeder.

A good breeder takes pride in the way they house their stock. They will ask you to visit their kennel so that you get to see the conditions that the dogs live in. Quite frankly, they have nothing to hide. This presents the perfect opportunity to check out how a breeder treats its dogs and puts you in a position to weed out those who aren't responsible enough.

A good breeder should have clean kennels that are well maintained. There may be a bit of cleaning or fixing here and there but this is usually unavoidable. However, there must not be any sign of outright neglect and filthy facilities.

Good breeders take the time to socialize their puppies so that they are ready for human interaction. *If you walk toward a litter of pups and they are all nervous around you, then it shows that the breeder hasn't socialized them properly.* Take this as a warning sign.

If you also notice that the adult dogs and puppies don't look healthy, friendly, or have temperament issues, do not buy from that breeder.

Perform Regular Health Checks

A good breeder will ensure that every dog they have routinely goes through a battery of tests prior to being used

Chapter Two: Choosing and Acquiring a Shiba Inu

for breeding. Any dog that shows signs of having a genetic disease will be spayed or neutered to prevent them from passing on the defective genes. The aim of a good breeder is always to improve the gene pool and minimize anything that may harm successive generations.

Don't be fooled by any breeder who gives you a verbal guarantee that their dogs have been cleared by a vet. Ask them to show you the health certificates and then verify the information. You can confirm the certificate by phone or online.

When looking for a Shiba Inu puppy, *the two main certificates that you should ask to see are hip dysplasia clearance and clear eyes certificates.*

Apart from certificates, a good breeder should be able to answer any questions you may have regarding genetic diseases common to Shiba Inus. An unethical breeder, however, will not want to discuss such issues because they aren't really concerned about them. They just want money to change hands as fast as possible. If a breeder seems uncomfortable answering your questions, don't buy from them.

Continual Advice and Support

A good breeder wants every puppy to get a good home. Therefore, they will take the time to explain all the information you need to raise the puppy the right way. This is not just something that they do before you buy. A good breeder will advise you throughout your dog's life.

Chapter Two: Choosing and Acquiring a Shiba Inu

No matter how simple or complex the question may be, they will always try to give the best answer possible. They will provide training, dietary, and health advice, and if necessary, put you in touch with organizations that can help you further.

In fact, there are some breeders who will go the extra mile and guarantee to take the puppy back in case of any unmanageable health issues. Some will even accept to take the dog in case your personal situation changes and you can no longer keep your Shiba Inu. An unethical breeder would never even dream of providing these kinds of services.

Questions to Ask a Shiba Inu Breeder

Now that you are aware of what separates a responsible breeder from an unethical one, here is a starting list of questions that you need to ask a breeder. A good breeder always expects a buyer to have questions and they should be prepared to answer them.

1. **Do you engage in Shiba Inu field trials or shows?** Most responsible breeders take part in field trials and shows. This is how you determine how serious the breeder is with his dogs. However, don't discount a breeder just because they aren't involved in such activities. Keep asking them more questions.

2. **Do you breed other dogs apart from Shiba Inus?** This is a way of identifying whether a breeder is mass producing a variety of breeds for money or sticking to a few breeds that they actually love. A

Chapter Two: Choosing and Acquiring a Shiba Inu

breeder who breeds maybe one or two breeds is good to work with. Though a breeder who is keeping three different breeds is also okay, anything more than that should be a warning sign.

3. **Have you registered the sire, dam, and their puppies?** When buying a pedigree dog, you have to ensure that they are registered. A good breeder will register their dogs and hand over the relevant paperwork when you come to pick up your puppy.

4. **Where do you raise your Shiba Inu puppies?** The best answer you can expect to hear is *in the home*. However, sometimes puppies are kept in kennels and still receive the necessary socialization and care. Ideally, you want a puppy that is used to receiving human attention and socialized with other animals.

5. **What level of breeding experience do you have?** This is a way of finding out how long they have been breeding Shiba Inus. You want to buy from someone who has the right amount of experience with Shiba Inus rather than an inexperienced breeder. At the same time, ask them how many litters they have bred. A breeder who has 15 years of experience but has only bred two Shiba Inu litters is not qualified, while one who has only two years of experience but has bred 15 litters is only doing it for the money. The number of years has to be proportional to the number of litters bred.

Chapter Two: Choosing and Acquiring a Shiba Inu

6. **Can you show me health certificates for the sire and dam?** A good breeder will never breed a dog that has health problems. They care too much about the kind of life their puppies will live. If a breeder is unable to produce any genuine health certificates, don't buy from them.

7. **Are there any inherited diseases in the lineage of this puppy?** You cannot avoid certain genetic diseases that are inherent in Shiba Inus. Instead of lying to you and saying that the puppy has no likelihood of developing any diseases, a good breeder will explain all potential ailments.

8. **If I am not able to care for my dog, will you take him back?** Most responsible breeders won't have a problem taking back the dog and will guarantee this agreement in writing but this will vary. On the other hand, don't let this be a deal breaker if the breeder ticks all the other boxes.

9. **Can I reach out to you in case I have any questions or issues with the dog?** There's no other acceptable answer here except a resounding "yes".

10. **When can I take the puppy home with me?** An unethical breeder will be quick to offload the puppy even before it reaches eight weeks of age. This is a cruel thing to do and may lead to behavioral problems in the future. A puppy should only be separated from its mother and siblings after eight weeks because it is still learning and developing social interaction.

Chapter Two: Choosing and Acquiring a Shiba Inu

11. **Can I see the parents?** A breeder should have the dam on site, so you should be able to meet at least one parent. Assess the temperament and appearance of the parents so that you know what to expect from your puppy in the future. If the sire is not available, ask the breeder to give you the contacts of the owner. You can then set up a meeting to view the father and verify its health certificates.

12. **Can you give me the contacts of people who've adopted Shiba Inu puppies from you?** You may want to talk to other owners who have adopted puppies from the breeder. They will tell you the condition of their dog and how the breeder has been engaging with them after the sale.

Questions from a Shiba Inu Breeder

Now that you have asked the breeder questions, it's time for you to answer some of your own. A good breeder will not sell you their dog without asking you some personal questions. Remember that their job is to take care of the welfare of their puppies, so they have to make sure that they are selling to someone who is competent enough to own a dog.

Here are a few examples of what you may be asked by a breeder:

1. **What are you looking for in a dog?** This is meant to see whether a Shiba Inu is the right breed for you.

Chapter Two: Choosing and Acquiring a Shiba Inu

2. **Can you bear the costs of owning a dog?** The breeder wants to know whether you are able to pay for food, toys, equipment, health care, and any medical emergencies.

3. **What kind of house do you live in?** The breeder wants to find out whether you live in an apartment or stand-alone house, with or without a garden, fenced or unfenced yard. This is a way of assessing how you will be able to ensure the dog gets enough fresh air and exercise every day.

4. **Where will the puppy sleep?** This is to check whether you have allocated a specific place for the dog or you'll simply toss in the backyard.

5. **How much time will you spend with your puppy?** Again, this is to check if you intend to pay adequate attention to the puppy or how long the puppy may be left alone.

6. **Are you already a dog owner?** The breeder is testing your experience with dogs. If you already own one, they need to know whether your current dog will be well-matched with a Shiba Inu.

7. **Do you have a spouse and/or kids?** The breeder wants to know whether there are other people who will be interacting with the dog in the home. Don't be surprised if you are asked to come with your family so that the breeder can see how everyone engages with the puppy.

Chapter Two: Choosing and Acquiring a Shiba Inu

Do not take these questions personally. This is all part of dealing with a breeder who cares about both his puppy and you as well.

You should also know that most breeders have long waiting lists when it comes to adopting Shiba Inu puppies. A good breeder first finds a good home for a Shiba Inu puppy and then starts breeding. This ensures that every puppy finds a home where they will live comfortably.

If you were expecting to engage in a quick transaction, you had better find another source for your puppy. You need to be patient when buying a Shiba Inu from a good breeder. The slow processes that have been put in place are meant to eliminate any impulsive buyers who may be ignorant of what it takes to properly raise a Shiba Inu.

Buying from a good breeder may not be fast, but if you are looking for good quality Shiba Inu puppy, the wait is definitely worth it!

Finally, if you want to find good breeders, check the online database of your national kennel club (AKC, UKC, etc.). You can also ask your local Shiba Inu Club to provide a listing of its recommended breeders.

Chapter Two: Choosing and Acquiring a Shiba Inu

Chapter Three: Preparing for Your Shiba Inu

Supplies and Equipment Needed

From the start of this book, you probably expected me to get to the training part right away. But I know that a lot of readers will be new dog parents. If you have ever owned a dog, then you probably already know how to train one. If you never have, it means you are a new dog parent, and you need as much helpful information as you can get. It may not be immediately apparent, but things such as choosing the right puppy and providing everything your Shiba Inu needs are pertinent to how smooth and seamless the training process turns out with a new puppy. This is mainly why I chose to

Chapter Three: Preparing for Your Shiba Inu

start the book with chapters on how you can select the right puppy. Having said this, let's look at the complete checklist of things you need for a new canine companion in a new home.

Few things are as exciting as the prospects to bring a brand-new puppy into your home. But before you take your new puppy home, you have to make sure that you are indeed ready to accommodate the new pup in your home. In other words, you have to make your house a prepared space for him. Puppies require a lot of dedication, attention, and care, so having a checklist of their essential needs is a great place to begin. Never forget that you don't need everything for a new puppy; you only need the basics and essentials.

Here are puppy essentials to have ready before welcoming a new pooch into your home.

Quality Puppy Food

Up until your new puppy clocks a year, he will need a constant supply of high-quality puppy food formulated specifically for a dog of his age, size, and development. Puppy foods are specifically important because they contain more nutrients than older dogs' food, and your puppy will need these special nutrients and nourishment to grow and develop at the right pace. If you got your dog from a breeder, you might come home with a supply of the food his breeder feeds to him. Either way, make sure you continue to provide him with the same diet he was weaned onto when he reaches your home. Any changes you want to make to the diet should be a gradual process. Talk to your vet if you are uncertain when or how to change to a new diet. Also, be sure to get food that is formulated specially to aid his rapid development into adulthood.

Food and Water Bowls

Food and water bowls are no-brainers when making a list of what to get your new puppy. The best kinds of bowls are the ceramic or stainless-steel types that are quite easier to clean. They also don't retain bacteria as plastic bowls do. Plus, ceramic and stainless-steel bowls are suitable for the dishwasher, and there are tons of beautiful designs to choose from.

Crate or Puppy Pad

You can choose to crate-train your new pup or use puppy pads with him. Either way, you will need something to keep your pet's urine or feces off your floors. I recommend crate-training, and you will find out about the best crate-training techniques as you read the book further. Be aware that you need to make your puppy's crate a safe and comfortable space. So, consider lining the base of the crate with soft bedding materials and make sure you keep your pet's favorite toy whenever he is in there. Puppy pads are also beneficial; they help to absorb moisture, which prevents leaks and odors. Perhaps the best thing about puppy pads is that they don't give room for urine to spread along with the parts.

Treats and Chews

Chapter Three: Preparing for Your Shiba Inu

Treats are puppy essentials, and they are particularly important for training. Without a ready bag of treats, training your puppy will be harder than normal, if not impossible. Treats simply make the job easier on you and your puppy. Since treats will be a regular part of your training tools, you must get the healthiest ones possible. Also, make sure the treats are soft and easy for your dog's tiny teeth to chew on. If you have never owned a puppy, be ready to have your new one chew your household items, including furniture, shoes, clothes, hands, and feet. Getting a good dog chew will help keep your puppy busy while redirecting his attention away from your household objects until he matures and becomes rid of his puppy teeth.

Dog Toys

Puppies play a lot, and it is your responsibility to keep your pup entertained. Entertainment helps keep the untrained pooch from becoming bored and, ultimately, destructive. You must get several toys of different textures available before you bring your new dog into your home. According to the American Kennel Club, the right number of toys for a new dog should be between 5 and 6. This way, you can interchange the toys a dog plays with while ensuring that you keep him on paws at all times. Apart from keeping your puppy engaged and active, toys also help with teething and chewing problems. However, before getting the toy, ensure it is a plush choice. More importantly, take it with you to the shelter or rescue to rub on littermates and parents to bring back their scent to your family home. This will help your dog settle in quickly with the rest of the family.

Chapter Three: Preparing for Your Shiba Inu

Leash, Collar, and Harness

A leash, collar, and harness are essential puppy wears that you will certainly have a lot of fun picking out. But it's not just about the fun; make sure you choose the right picks for your puppy. A new puppy isn't used to "wearing" things, so pick out a collar that is soft, plush, and adjustable – something that won't irritate his neck or weigh down on him. Remember that you will have to go through many collars as your puppy grows and matures. For now, get the type that matches his needs. When choosing a leash, get one that is like 4 to 6 feet long. Note that your first few walks with your dog are going to be quite intriguing and fascinating since your puppy usually won't know what a leash is or why you are attaching it to him. And, because your puppy, whether it is of a large breed or small one, will be quite small, it helps to attach a harness instead of a leash to his collars. When there is too much pressure on the throat, a puppy might experience what we call tracheal collapse and possibly other injuries. Get a soft, adjustable harness ready for your new friend and keep the leash for when he becomes older.

Puppy Playpen

You don't want your puppy wandering around the house while he is still undergoing training. One thing about puppies is that they are just like toddlers; they have no idea how to potty and have to be trained. Without training, they will pretty much go wherever they please. Not to mention that they will also be chewing and destroying things they find

Chapter Three: Preparing for Your Shiba Inu

around them. When left unsupervised, you will need to make sure that they are restricted to a certain safe area where their actions and behaviors are contained. So, when you are about to start puppy-proofing and potty training, you might want to think about getting a puppy playpen where you can keep your pooch and contain him.

Puppy Gate

A puppy gate (baby gate) is crucial to the training stage and process. At first, you will need to puppy-proof your house because of the new pet. Understandably, you may have certain areas where you don't want your puppy to reach, such as the kitchen, the basement, or the living room where you have your newly purchased, sparkly, new rug. Consider going for a retractable gate that you can keep away while it's not needed.

Bedding

Just as you would for babies, keep your pup warm and snuggly during bedtimes and naptimes. Make sure the material of your puppy's bedding is soft and gentle, yet easy to wash. Regardless of the type of puppy bedding you purchase, make sure you have extra bedding that you can use interchangeably in your puppy's crate and playpen. Keep in mind that you can take the bedding and blanket to rub on your pooch's littermates before putting it in the crate or playpen. Doing this will make your dog feel more comfortable in his first few nights with you.

Chapter Three: Preparing for Your Shiba Inu

Grooming Brush and Combs

Your dog will require regular brushing and combing of his coat to keep him looking healthy and beautiful. Depending on your puppy's breed, you may require special brushes and combs to maintain a well-groomed coat. Without these, his fur and coat can become knotted in just a few days with you. A soft-bristled brush is the ideal type of grooming brush for daily brushing and grooming of your pet's coat. If your pet has longer hair than most, use a metal comb.

Puppy Shampoo and Conditioner

Along with grooming brush and comb, you will need to get gentle and standard puppy shampoo and conditioner. Keep in mind that you should never use human shampoo or conditioner for your pet. Also, you shouldn't use an adult dog shampoo for a puppy. Find an all-natural pet shampoo specially formulated for puppies that not only cleans your dog's fur but also feels gentle on his delicate skin and fur.

Nail Trimmer

A quality dog nail trimmer is essential for any puppy or dog. Don't be surprised to find that your puppy has needle-like nails, and his nails grow as fast as weeds. Unless you have enough money to visit a professional groomer once every week for regular nail trimming, you will want to get a quality nail trimmer that is sure to get the job done. Ask an expert how short to trim your pet's nails because trimming too fast can lead to a quick injury, resulting in bleeding, infection, and pain for your pup. However, don't be scared of trimming as not cutting and cleaning your canine friend's nails could also result in infection and pain. Get a nail trimmer that has a quick sensor to alert you when you are close to trimming too short. This should help eliminate any feeling of fear you might have about harming your pet.

Conclusively, while thinking of the things you need for your new puppy, you should remember to ask yourself what your puppy needs from you. Your new puppy will need you to be consistent and patient with him at all times, but especially while he is undergoing training. Consistent training is the key to raising a healthy, well-behaved, and happy puppy that is obedient and willing to socialize.

Dog-proofing Your Home

Dogs are inquisitive creatures and will likely explore places in your home that you forgot even existed. Here's a quick guide on protecting your dog and home from one and other.

Tip: The first thing you should know is that even if you wrap everything in your house in protective plastic and then coat it in Teflon twice your dog is still going to find something to gnaw at or pee on, especially if young.

Please be patient with them and remember that this is part and parcel of training a dog. There will always be a bit of collateral damage, but here's how you can limit it:

Chapter Three: Preparing for Your Shiba Inu

- *Tidy Up*: It seems obvious but the best thing you can do to stop your dog destroying things is to simply move them out of reach. Spend time clearing away clutter regularly and pay special attention to ensuring small things which they could swallow are completely out of reach. Having a tidy home will actually help your dog learn faster too, as there will be less visual stimulation to distract them from training.
- *Electricals*: Dogs explore with their mouths so wires and other electrical appliances pose a big threat to their wellbeing. Make sure all wires are flush to the wall and wrapped in protective sleeves. Unplugging things and turning the sockets off when not in use will also make sure your friend stays safe.
- *Plants*: If you have plants indoors or out, perform a quick check to ensure you don't have any poisonous species which he or she could ingest.
- *Chemicals & Cosmetics*: Curious dogs can often find their way into cabinets and cupboards, so it's a good idea to fit low doors with childproof latches.
- *Food:* Many human foods such as chocolate or those high in sugar or fat can be harmful to dogs, so be sure to keep these well out of reach. You should also keep your dog's food hidden as if they uncover it they could eat themselves sick.
- *Trash & Bin Bags*: Get used to cleaning up as you go along as leaving things even for a small amount of time could give your dog an opportunity to get into them and harm themselves with whatever nasty things are within.

Chapter Three: Preparing for Your Shiba Inu

- *Bolt Holes*: Dogs are explorers by nature so make sure you don't leave doors or windows open. If you have a cat flap keep that secure too. It's also important to go out into the yard and check for any holes in the fencing, although you should never leave them alone there anyway.
- *Ponds or Pools:* If your dog can make their way into deep water then you need to ensure they can make their way out, too. Train them to swim and climb out as soon as you are able to do so and never leave them unattended in this area.
- *Boundaries*: Use baby gates to close off areas such as stairwells and bedrooms to keep your dog from accessing them. We will learn how to reinforce these rules later.

Above all just use common sense when dog-proofing your home. If something looks like it could pose a threat to their wellbeing then deal with it. You can never be too careful.

Chapter Four: Feeding Your Shiba Inu

Now, let's move on to one of the most important aspects of caring for your Shiba Inu – his diet. You have to know exactly what you should feed your puppy as such will ensure that you will be giving him the right foods all the time, particularly those that meet his nutritional requirements and needs based on his age, activity level, and lifestyle.

Your Shiba Inu will only be able to bring out his incredible personality if you give him all the nutrients that his small and adorable body needs. This chapter will cover some of the suggested foods that can perfectly meet the requirements of all Shiba Inu regardless of their actual size and shape.

You will also get an idea about how much you should feed this breed to prevent them from overeating. Basically, almost all things that you have to know about the Shiba Inu diet form part of this chapter.

How Much Food Does Your Shiba Inu Need?

Before starting to buy dog foods that are perfect for the Shiba Inu, it is crucial to learn more about nutrition so you can provide him with what his body needs exactly. One important point you should remember, in this case, is the fact that he is pretty little. Since this breed only weighs around 17 to 23 lbs., the food he needs to eat is a bit lower compared to larger dog breeds.

However, you should constantly remind yourself about the importance of finding the perfect balance between too little and too much. It is the key to ensuring that your dog will receive enough food and nutrition. In most cases, a typical 17-lb. Shiba Inu puppy who has a normal activity level requires around 342 kcal daily.

However, if the Shiba Inu is more energetic and active, then you may need to provide him with more foods – up to 545 kcal daily. This should be enough to keep up with his higher activity level. Once he gets older, you can also expect his active personality to dwindle a bit.

He will become a bit less active, which can prompt you to lessen his kibble to around 280 kcal daily. Also, remember that these dogs are small, which means that you do not have

Chapter Four: Feeding Your Shiba Inu

to feed them too much. It is even crucial to regulate and control their meals to prevent them from overeating.

Essential Nutrients Needed by the Shiba Inu

Your Shiba Inu needs certain nutrients for him to thrive and grow into a healthy and happy dog. With that said, you have to make sure that the foods you feed him offer a good supply of the following nutrients:

Protein

Just like when protein is vital for every human being, it is also crucial for the health of your Shiba Inu. A higher amount of protein is even needed especially for more active consumers. It plays a crucial role in developing muscle mass. One thing to note about the protein or amino acid is that it can either be plant-based or animal-based.

If you have a Shiba Inu, the animal-based one is a better option. Aside from being healthier for them compared to the plant-based ones, animal-based protein is also easier to digest for them. With that said, pick dog foods mainly based on meat, such as turkey, whole chicken, fish, mutton, beef, duck, bison, or venison.

Most Shiba Inu dogs crave such food items the most. If you intend to buy commercial dog foods with the mentioned varieties of meat, then make sure to read the labels carefully.

Chapter Four: Feeding Your Shiba Inu

Find the major and main ingredients. Go for those marked to have animal-based protein specifically.

Healthy Fats

Your Shiba Inu also needs a good supply of healthy fats. Despite being classified as healthy fats, they are not around to trigger weight gain on your Shiba Inu. They are even critical for the overall health of your puppy, provided you only supply them in moderate amounts. The good thing about letting your pup ingest sufficient amounts of healthy fats is that they can support their active and energetic personality.

The essential fats in their foods can supply them with sufficient energy that will help them have all the energy they need for the whole day. Apart from being supportive of their energy and active lifestyle, healthy fats are also crucial in maintaining the good health and shine of the thick double coat of your Shiba Inu.

As much as possible, supply your puppy with animal-based fats, such as fish oil. The reason is that they are the healthiest versions of fat for dogs that can also promote better heart health. Moreover, these fats are easier for the liver and metabolism of your dog. Just make sure to keep each portion small and retain sufficient calorie consumption so your pet can get the most out of these fats.

Do not forget to check the label of the food products, too. Ensure that the label states for animal sources, such as fats taken from chicken fat or salmon oil. They are among

Chapter Four: Feeding Your Shiba Inu

those that the body of your dog can easily absorb. You may also want to use plant oils as they can balance Omega-3 and Omega-6 – both of which are essential fats you can often find in various dog food products and recipes.

Carbohydrates

Carbohydrate is also a key nutrient in a Shiba Inu diet. One reason is that your Shiba Inu needs carbs in order to sustain the energy required by his lively personality. Keep in mind, though, that the key is moderation. You should still avoid feeding him too much as excessive amounts of carbs may hamper his health. In low to moderate amounts, these carbs will be vital to his overall health as such nutrients contribute to the elevation of his energy.

Complex carbs should compose a minimum of 25% of the food consumed by your Shiba Inu. Some sources of these complex carbs are whole grains, legumes, beans, and veggies. These are the carbs that can supply your dog with the energy or speed he needs to perform playful and active activities and finish his chores. Also, ensure that you get carbs from digestible sources while preventing the protein content from getting too high. It should only be a max of 5%.

Fiber

Your beloved Shiba Inu also needs a good supply of fiber. It is highly recommended for around 5% of his daily diet to contain fiber. This nutrient is essential for the life of your Shiba Inu as it can maintain the strength, good health, and

Chapter Four: Feeding Your Shiba Inu

efficiency of his gut. Apart from creating the necessary bulk in your puppy's intestines and stomach, fiber is also essential in smoothing out the pooping process.

Other Essential Vitamins and Minerals

Your Shiba Inu also needs some of the vitamins and minerals present in other foods, particularly in fruits and veggies. You can even find a lot of companies that primarily manufacture foods adding supplements to their products to increase their power and nutrition content.

When shopping for food for your Shiba Inu, some of the vitamins you should look for are Vitamin A, Vitamin C, Vitamin D, and Vitamin E. Such vitamins are crucial for the health of your puppy as they can protect him from various diseases, like those linked to his muscles, eyes, and bones.

What the Shiba Inu Diet Should Not Contain?

While certain nutrients should be present in the daily diet of your Shiba Inu, there are also those that should be avoided. Ensure that the foods you feed your Shiba Inu do not contain any of the following as they may put them in danger:

- Raw Foods – The majority of raw foods, especially raw meat, are not good for the health of your puppy. With that said, ensure that his diet does not contain such raw ingredients or products. Aside from causing an upset stomach, these raw foods

Chapter Four: Feeding Your Shiba Inu

may also hamper the oral and dental health of your puppy.

- Excess Sugar – Just like humans, sugar is also one of those food ingredients and items that can cause harm to your puppy. With that in mind, you should avoid giving your Shiba Inu too much of it. You can give him fruits recognized for containing sugar but ensure that you do so in moderation. That way, you can prevent your puppy from consuming too much sugar that is bad for his overall health.

- Artificial Preservatives – You also have to be extra careful when preparing the diet of your Shiba Inu so you can prevent them from ingesting harmful artificial preservatives, like BHA and BHT. These artificial preservatives are notorious for being toxic to pets, particularly dogs. With that in mind, you have to ensure that the food products you are buying do not contain them.

- Additives – Check the additives integrated into the dog food products you intend to buy or use for your homemade dog food recipes. Some additives you should avoid using are taste enhancers, colorings, preservatives, and flavorings as they can trigger the development of major ailments, such as cancer.

By ensuring that what you feed your Shiba Inu does not contain any of these harmful and toxic ingredients, you have an assurance that his health and body will continue to be in tip-top shape.

Basics of Feeding the Shiba Inu

One fact about the Shiba Inu that matters a lot when it comes to feeding him is his people-centric attitude. His people-centric nature is one reason why you can expect him to be devoted to you so it is highly likely that he will always look for you for his basic feeding needs. Also, be aware that most Shiba Inu dogs are insistent. With that attitude, there is a great possibility that he will nibble, nip, and beg for food throughout the day.

Fortunately, this breed is also capable of sending signals in terms of the ideal feeding schedule. However, the curious nature of the Shiba Inu will also cause him to just take one or two bites, come back to you to grab your attention, then go back to his food. It would be like he is asking for a feeding buddy. If this scenario happens, then remember that it is normal. Do not reprimand him for it or discourage him from doing so, unless this behavior gets overboard that it tends to become annoying.

As far as the feeding schedule is concerned, your Shiba Inu puppy will most likely need feeding around three to four times daily. The rule of thumb would be giving him around one-fourth cup of his food during mealtimes. Also, do not forget to take away his food bowl after around fifteen to

Chapter Four: Feeding Your Shiba Inu

twenty minutes as this will serve as his encouragement to eat faster.

You should also follow these guidelines based on what stage of life he is in:

- Puppy – Just like what has been mentioned a while ago, a Shiba Inu puppy needs to eat at least 3 to 4 times daily. His small size prevents him from consuming the required amount of food in just one to two meals so you should try to divide it into 3 to 4 smaller meals.

Also, make sure that your Shiba Inu puppy receives around 8% crude fat and a minimum of 22% crude protein daily. This is essential for his healthy growth and development. You should also remember that the active and alert personality of your Shiba Inu also means that his metabolism works fast.

Taking that into account, you should offer nutritious foods that are not heavy on his tiny stomach. One way to handle this is to go for a dog food brand, which manufactures products specifically for the toy or small breeds.

- Adult – Your Shiba Inu puppy can be considered as an adult upon reaching twelve months. When he reaches this age, you can transition him to a form of diet specifically made for adult toy dog breeds. One thing you may notice in the labels of adult dog foods that are compatible with the needs of the Shiba Inu is the consistently high protein ratio.

Chapter Four: Feeding Your Shiba Inu

However, you will also notice a reduction in the calorie content as it aims to prevent the dog from becoming overweight or obese. You do not have to worry about this lower calorie content. Remember that the dog food is already good for your dog provided it contains added supplements, such as chondroitin and glucosamine that can strengthen joints and improve his immunity.

- Senior – Your Shiba Inu will probably hit his senior stage upon 7 to 8 years old. It is the time when he begins to slow down. Once he reaches this stage, you have to pay closer attention to his daily diet. You need to make sure that you provide him with foods that can help him even as he gets a bit slower.

Also, note that reaching the senior stage means that his once healthy metabolism will begin to falter. The health of his teeth, joints, and bones will be affected, too. In that case, remember that you do not have to lessen his food consumption that much. You should set a goal of making his diet as nutritious as possible.

Find a food formula, which takes into account the specific requirements of a senior toy dog breed. With such a food formula, you can expect your Shiba Inu to receive all the nutrients he needs without worrying about him gaining excessive pounds.

One more thing you should remember is that once your Shiba Inu becomes a senior, two or three meals daily is enough. Do not forget to check the instructions on the food package so you will get a clear idea of how much you should

Chapter Four: Feeding Your Shiba Inu

feed your dog based on his age. Avoid unnecessarily increasing the recommended dose as it may only lead to excess weight or obesity.

Is it Safe to Feed a Shiba Inu Human Food?

When it comes to creating the proper diet plan for your Shiba Inu, one question that may have crossed your mind is whether or not it is safe to feed this breed with human food. The answer is it depends on what you feed him. Yes, the Shiba Inu breed can eat human food but you have to make sure that you pick the most sensible food choices – those that are not toxic and harmful for your dog specifically.

Also, remember that just like you, your Shiba Inu also needs to consume a balanced diet, so you should be extra careful and wise in selecting the human foods that you intend to feed him. It is the key to optimizing his health regardless of age. This is also the principle followed by most dog food companies. All of them are already aware of the right balance of nutrients, fats, minerals, proteins, as well as other ingredients and elements capable of improving the health of dogs.

With that, buying from them may be the most sensible choice for you. However, this does not mean you cannot feed your dog with whatever you and your family are eating. It would be best to wait for your Shiba Inu to become an adult before feeding him human food, though. You should avoid

Chapter Four: Feeding Your Shiba Inu

feeding your Shiba Inu puppy human food as he is still in the developing stage.

His digestive system is not also ready to take in the foods of humans considering the fact that it is still in the stage of development. Feed him the foods recommended for him during this early stage so you can help in boosting his growth until he reaches adulthood.

Once your Shiba Inu grows into an adult, you can finally let him enjoy the foods you are eating. Just make sure that you are already completely aware of what foods are safe and non-toxic for him. Some safe food choices for your adult Shiba Inu are:

- Boiled chicken – It is probably the easiest food you can prepare for your dog. You can also expect him to love it. Choose the boneless skin-on thigh when boiling as it has the perfect balance of delicious taste and good nutrients. However, if your dog has issues with excess weight, then you should consider boiling skinless and boneless chicken breast for him as it is healthier.

- Hard-boiled egg – Another great idea would be a hard-boiled egg, which is a great way to make your Shiba Inu get protein. Give him just half of the egg, though, since the protein here is not as easily digestible as that derived from meat.

- Steamed or boiled vegetable – You can also offer your adult Shiba Inu a serving or two of steamed or boiled vegetables. What is great about this food option is that it lets him receive sufficient fiber. The majority of boiled vegetables actually work great for the Shiba Inu breed but you should still make sure that the veggies you are feeding him do not have even the slightest sign of harm to him.

Among the safest vegetables you can feed your Shiba Inu are red tomatoes, green beans, carrots, and pumpkin. Avoid cabbage, cauliflower, and broccoli as they tend to cause some potential issues in the health of the Shiba Inu. Make sure that you do not feed garlic, green tomato, and onion to him as those are proven harmful for dogs.

- Homemade biscuits – It is also very rewarding to prepare homemade biscuits for your dog. Fortunately, it is not that hard to make them nowadays as you can find several recipes online. When preparing biscuits, though, make sure that you lower the butter and sugar content. This is to prevent your dog from gaining too much weight, which may result in health problems later on.

- Apple – Apple is also healthy for dogs. You can offer half of one apple to your dog so he can receive its benefits. Just make sure that you take off the core of the apple as well as its seeds as those may be toxic to your dog plus they are kind of hard to digest. Once you have removed the harmful parts of the apple, you will have peace of mind feeding him with it as it can supply him with plenty of nutrients that are good for his health, including Vitamin C, fiber, and potassium.

Chapter Four: Feeding Your Shiba Inu

- Banana – This fruit is also safe for your Shiba Inu to eat. You can give one-half of a piece of banana if you notice your dog hungrier than usual. It could be because he spent too much of his energy on exercise or when playing. Just a bit of it can already make him feel full plus it has fiber.

If you want to give your Shiba Inu the chance to try other types of food apart from the usual commercial dog foods, then you can let him taste the ones that humans eat. Just make sure to research those foods that are 100 percent safe and non-toxic for your dog, so you will never put him at risk.

Chapter Five: Grooming Your Shiba Inu

Grooming is not just an important part of keeping your puppy fun to snuggle and looking cute—it's also important for their overall health and a great way to build trust with body handling. This section will cover basic grooming recommendations to keep your puppy's skin, coat, teeth, and nails in tip-top shape.

Skin and Coat

Chapter Five: Grooming Your Shiba Inu

Your puppy's coat is what most people associate with "grooming"—but there's much more to it than that. This section will cover the considerations you need to take when caring for the health, integrity, and appearance of your puppy's coat and skin.

Types of Coat

Did you know that though most dogs have fur, some have hair? Hair, which is more like the hair humans have, has a longer growing cycle, meaning it sheds less frequently. It's also smoother and finer to the touch, but it traps dirt more easily (partly due to the less frequent shedding), which can easily result in tangles and mats. Dogs with continuously growing hair (such as shih tzus or Yorkshire terriers) and curly-coated breeds (such as poodles and Portuguese water dogs) require regular trimming by a groomer to keep their coats at a manageable and healthy length. They may also need their faces trimmed now and then to prevent their hair from getting in their eyes and obscuring their vision.

Dogs with a "double coat," like Shiba Inus, have not one but two layers of fur: an undercoat and a topcoat. The topcoat acts as a guard, repelling water, and the undercoat serves as an insulating layer. People sometimes mistakenly believe they should shave double-coated dogs to prevent mats or keep them cool in hot weather. Never do this! Shaving a double-coated dog does not help keep them cool; it just damages the topcoat. The way to maintain a healthy, clean double coat is to regularly brush it, trimming only the long hairs by the legs, bums, tails, and feet, if needed.

Chapter Five: Grooming Your Shiba Inu

Brushing and Combing

Brushing your puppy has numerous benefits, including removing tangles, dead hair, and dead skin cells; stimulating the skin's surface; and distributing natural skin oils. Brushing can even be relaxing for some dogs, much like a massage, and can be a great bonding experience for you and your puppy. Remember to make your puppy's first encounters with brushing positive by using treats! One brush stroke equals one treat. Gradually increase the number of brush strokes before you feed a treat as your puppy accepts the handling.

How often you brush your puppy will really depend on its coat type. Short-haired breeds, such as Dobermans and dalmatians, do fine with once-weekly brushing, whereas long-coated breeds, like retrievers and spaniels, benefit from daily grooming to maintain tangle-free tresses. Leaving your dog's coat unbrushed for too long can result in painfully tight mats that may require shaving, professional grooming, or even grooming under sedation. Regular maintenance is key!

There are multiple types of brushes available for dog grooming, and much like the frequency of brushing, the type you select will depend largely on your puppy's coat. A brush might be designed to remove mats or tangles, clear out loose fur from the undercoat, or maintain the topcoat. At the store, ask for help selecting a brush if you're not sure you have the right type, or book an appointment with a professional groomer to learn some more tips specific to your dog's needs.

Chapter Five: Grooming Your Shiba Inu

Here are some of the most common types of brushes available.

- **Bristle brushes** are the most versatile. Pick a brush with shorter, denser bristles for short-coated dogs and longer, more spaced-out bristles for long-coated dogs. These brushes remove dirt and loose hair and stimulate the skin.

- **Slicker brushes** are designed to remove loose hair and dirt but will also remove tangles and some mats from short- to medium-length coats. Don't apply too much pressure, as the teeth could become uncomfortable.

- **Undercoat rakes and other "deshedding" tools** (like the Furminator) are designed to remove loose fur from the undercoat without damaging the healthy topcoat. Breeds like Shiba Inuss and huskies benefit greatly from these types of brushes, especially during spring and fall, when their coat is transitioning with the seasons. Make sure the length of the "pins" or teeth matches the length of your dog's fur—too short and you'll miss the inner layers of the undercoat, too long and you may irritate the skin.

To Pay or Not to Pay?

When does your puppy need to see a groomer? That depends on a few factors. How dirty is your dog? How capable are you of tackling the job? What type of coat does your puppy have, and does it need trimming? Groomers are professionals at tackling a dirty and disheveled dog coat. They have the proper tools on hand and are much more efficient at the job than you or I. Groomers don't just rid your

Chapter Five: Grooming Your Shiba Inu

dog's coat of dirt, debris, and tangles; they also thoroughly brush out any dead or loose hair, trim hair where required, and may clean your dog's ears and clip their nails. Long- or curly-coated breeds need to see a groomer more regularly, whereas some short-coated dogs may never need to see one at all, depending on your ability to maintain their skin and coat at home.

If your puppy will be making frequent groomer visits, introduce them to the experience in a positive way early on. Take several "fun trips" to the groomer—just go in and receive treats, with no actual grooming. A Fear Free Certified groomer will be patient and gentle-handed, and will ensure the first groom is a positive experience by only doing as much handling as your puppy will happily tolerate. Ask to stay and watch the appointment so you can pick up tips. You can also ask for homework to help your dog learn the necessary handling and get used to the different tools.

Bathing

How often should you give your puppy a bath? It really depends. If your dog starts to develop an odor, a bath is a good idea. A roll in a fresh mud puddle (or something worse)? Bath time! Most dogs do fine with baths a few times a year at most, and this is usually more for odor control than for coat or skin health. If your dog has a medical skin condition, your veterinarian may recommend frequent baths to help treat or manage this—but bathing your puppy too often can actually **cause** skin irritation by stripping the

Chapter Five: Grooming Your Shiba Inu

natural, healthy oils from their coat, so don't do this unless your vet specifically recommends it.

When bathing your puppy, use shampoos specifically formulated for dogs; human shampoos can irritate your dog's skin. Leftover shampoo can cause irritation, too, so rinse it out well. When you think you've rinsed enough, rinse once more to be sure!

How to Bathe Your Puppy

Introduce bathing to your puppy early on. As with any novel and potentially scary experience, it's important to make the experience positive and not overwhelming. You can do this by (a) breaking the process down into small, achievable steps, and (b) pairing baths with treats.

Start by bringing your puppy into the bathroom and feeding them 5 to 10 treats in a row before letting them leave the room. Do this multiple times, until your puppy is comfortable and confident in the space. Next, feed your puppy treats in the empty bathtub! (You can either lift them into the tub or encourage them to jump in themselves, whatever they're most comfortable with. Make sure you have a nonslip mat on the bottom of your tub so your puppy doesn't get scared or hurt.) Next, feed your puppy treats in a bathtub pre-filled with one inch of water. Gradually fill the tub up more each session and experiment with gently splashing your puppy. Slosh water up one leg, followed immediately by praise and treats. Only increase the amount of splashing and handling as your puppy is confident and comfortable.

Chapter Five: Grooming Your Shiba Inu

Teeth

Puppies require oral maintenance. Brushing their teeth daily is the best way to manage plaque and tartar buildup, just like in humans. Once-a-week brushing is not as ideal, but it's still far superior to no brushing at all, so do what you can to give your puppy's teeth adequate attention. Use a toothpaste created for dogs, as human toothpastes may contain ingredients that are toxic to dogs. Dog toothpaste also comes in flavors that appeal to them more, such as chicken and beef. Toothbrushes designed for dogs are easier to use than human toothbrushes, with smaller heads that fit their mouths. You can also purchase a rubber finger toothbrush that you put on like a finger puppet for ease of use.

There are many dental chews and treats on the market. Some use the act of chewing to help scrape plaque off teeth and stimulate healthy gums, while others are formulated with specific ingredients like enzymes that contribute to overall oral health. If you don't brush your puppy's teeth, these treats are better than nothing. Be mindful of the extra calories and feed them in moderation.

Your puppy's teeth should be examined for dental disease at every veterinary appointment. Smaller dogs are more prone to dental disease and generally need cleanings earlier and more frequently. Breeds like Chihuahuas commonly retain their baby teeth even after their adult teeth have come in, which can cause crowding and make it easier for plaque to build up. These teeth sometimes need to be extracted if they don't fall out on their own. Note that while your puppy is transitioning from baby to adult teeth, they lose their teeth just like humans do, so don't be alarmed if you find a bloody molar on the floor or blood on your puppy's chew toys during this time.

How to Brush Your Dog's Teeth

Much like bathing, you want to introduce toothbrushing to your dog early on, in a slow and positive way, repeating each step several times, until your dog is clearly comfortable and not avoiding the contact. Start by introducing your puppy to the toothbrush (without toothpaste), then touch the toothbrush to your puppy's cheek for five seconds. Next, show your puppy the toothbrush with toothpaste on it, which they can lick off if they want. Feed them a few treats at each step.

To get your puppy used to having their mouth handled, start by simply touching their muzzle for one second, feeding them a treat, and taking your hand away. Gradually increase how long you leave your hand on the muzzle, then cup your hand over the top of the muzzle, put gentle pressure on the muzzle, and so on, eventually opening the top of the mouth to expose the teeth. Again, feed a few treats at each step.

Now to start brushing! Start with one to two seconds of gentle brushing (followed by a treat, of course), and gradually increase the duration of brushing and the pressure applied.

Chapter Five: Grooming Your Shiba Inu

Nails

Regular nail trimming is important in order to keep your puppy's nails at a safe and healthy length. When they get too long, they reduce your dog's traction and cause abnormal paw placement when walking, which can result in strain on the supporting structures in the leg over time. Plus, long nails are at a higher risk of breaking, which can be painful.

I recommend weekly nail trims, which not only maintain a healthy nail length but also make the job a lot faster and easier to perform. Why? In the core of a dog's nail is something called the "quick," which supplies blood and nerves to the nail. Humans have it under our nails too — hence, the phrase "cut me to the quick." Just like with humans, a normal nail trim is painless. But if your puppy is crying, you might have cut their nails too short and hit the quick, which can be very painful (think of how much it hurts when your fingernail gets injured!) and can result in bleeding. Having styptic powder on hand will help stop the bleeding and reduce the pain if you do accidentally clip the quick. Place some styptic powder in the palm of your hand and gently press the bleeding nail into the powder for a minute or two to stop the bleeding.

There are many different nail trimming devices for dogs on the market. Nail clipper styles are a personal preference, so test them out in your hand before you purchase anything. Scissor clippers are good for bigger, thicker nails. Guillotine clippers work just as their name implies, with a wide blade that slides down through a set of grooves. A motorized Dremel nail grinder files down nails instead of clipping them, but be aware that the whirring noise might spook your puppy initially and long toe hairs can get caught in the machinery.

How to Clip Your Dog's Nails

Nail trims can be traumatic for many dogs, and some even need to be sedated for the procedure at a vet clinic. That's why early exposure and handling of the feet from a young age is so crucial. As with any new form of handling, start early and introduce nail clipping with patience and positivity. Reward your puppy with praise and treats for sniffing the clippers, then work up to touching the clippers to their body, starting with the shoulder and gradually working your way toward the upper leg, ankle, and eventually the paw. Expose your puppy to paw handling by first simply touching the paw, then gently holding it, then grasping it more firmly, feeding them treats all the while. Now incorporate the clippers. Start by holding the paw and touching the clippers to the nail, and work up to taking a snip! One nail equals one treat at the beginning. Keep your expectations realistic. Your puppy may only be comfortable having a few nails clipped, so be prepared to stop and try again the next day.

If you've never clipped a dog's nails before, I recommend getting a quick lesson from your puppy's groomer or veterinary team. They can show you how to evaluate the length of your puppy's quick and the appropriate angle at which to cut the nail.

Chapter Five: Grooming Your Shiba Inu

Eyes and Ears

Puppies' eyes and ears generally don't require frequent cleaning or grooming, but there are a few exceptions. As previously mentioned, some dogs require trimming to keep the hair on their face out of their eyes. Some white-colored dogs are also prone to pinkish or reddish-brown "tear stains" under their eyes, which are caused by porphyrins, a natural component of canine tears and saliva. To avoid staining, wipe under your puppy's eyes twice daily with a warm cloth to dilute and wash away the tears, starting close to the eye and moving outward. If you're worried your dog produces an excessive amount of tears, visit the vet to ensure there is no health condition that needs attention.

Compared to dogs with upright ears, dogs with droopy ears naturally have less airflow and more heat and moisture in their ears. This can become a breeding ground for bacteria, so check them regularly for redness, discharge, or an off-putting odor. If you're concerned about the amount of hair in your dog's ear canal, speak to your vet or groomer about trimming it to allow for more adequate circulation. If your dog is prone to ear debris or infections, your vet may prescribe regular cleaning using a safe over-the-counter or prescription ear-cleaning solution.

Chapter Five: Grooming Your Shiba Inu

Chapter Six: Training and Behavior Modification

Housebreaking Your Puppy

Next, it is time to look into housebreaking your Shiba Inu puppy. Puppies are not born knowing that they can only relieve themselves outside. However, they do have a natural inclination to avoid going in their beds. This can, unfortunately, end with your own bed being used as a potential area to relieve himself, if you do not train him, but thankfully, there are methods that you can learn to help eliminate those negative behaviors entirely.

Within this section, we are going to be diving into how to housebreak your puppy. No one wants to have puppy pee

Chapter Six: Training and Behavior Modification

and poo all over their home, so you will probably find that this is one of the first training exercises that you are going to be regularly pushing. You want to ensure that your pup is not going to have accidents all over your house, but you may not know where to begin. Thankfully, however, your resource for potty training or housebreaking your Shiba Inu dog is here.

What to Expect

Before you begin, please note that good potty training is not instantaneous—not even close. Potty training will take time, consistency, and patience. You cannot expect to see that your dog has become fully house trained for up to a year with some of the larger breeds that tend to develop a bit slower than their smaller counterparts. Because the various breeds of dogs are so incredibly different from pup to pup, it can be really difficult to know what to expect for your specific breed.

When you begin, you are going to find that you will need to take your pup out regularly. Smaller breeds, like Shiba Inus, will need to go out much more frequently than larger breeds just due to being smaller and therefore having smaller bladders and higher metabolisms. Both of these translate to going regularly. Larger breeds may be able to go just a bit longer than their smaller counterparts, but not by much during those early years.

As a general rule, a pup can hold its bladder for roughly one hour per year of age, plus one. However, in theory, that means that your 3-month-old dog will need you to take him out every four hours, even overnight when you

Chapter Six: Training and Behavior Modification

may otherwise want to be sleeping. You will need to do this to meet your pup's biological need to relieve itself.

In potty training, you are going to be best served learning to recognize your pet's cues and then taking him out every time you see them. Every time your pup does go outside, you will want to praise him or her heavily. You may even decide to tie some high-value treats to this activity—perhaps your pup gets a treat out of your pocket each time that he or she goes outside. In making sure that you are regularly reinforcing this behavior, you will find that your pup is much happier to go outside over time.

How to Housebreak Your Puppy

Housebreaking your Shiba Inu puppy is quite simple—it will just take lots of time, patience, and reinforcement before your pup entirely catches onto the process. All you have to do is follow the following steps:

- Keep your pup on a schedule regularly—there should be food at very specific times each day and then remove it when that time is up. This will help regulate out his or her metabolism.

- Take your pup out first thing in the morning and every hour during the time that you are potty training. Your pup may be able to hold it for longer, but it will not help him or her really train any better if you do and you run the risk of having more and more accidents that you are trying to avoid.

Chapter Six: Training and Behavior Modification

- Make sure that pup goes out right before bed each and every night.

- Take the pup to the same place in your yard each tie and encourage him or her to sniff around. The smell of previous waste will linger and encourage him to go there again. This is precisely why so many pups will have the same accident in the same places indoors—they can smell their waste there.

- Always praise when your pup goes outside, followed by a high-ticket treat at first. You may try going on a walk, for example, or playing with your pup after he or she has gone.

Crate Training

Some people find that they are happiest using a crate to train their Shiba Inu pups to go. This is because being confined in a crate activates your pup's natural instincts—they will not void where they sleep, and because you will be encouraging them to sleep in their crate, they are not likely to have accidents in there if they can avoid it at all. You will want to ensure that your pup is going out regularly, even if you keep him or her in a crate, and if you are crating, make sure that they are never in there longer than a couple of hours at a time.

With crate training, all you are going to do is place your pup in the crate for naps and when you are not actively supervising him or her. This can really help you make sure

Chapter Six: Training and Behavior Modification

that there are no accidents around the house. When you are crate training, keep the following factors in mind:

- Make sure that your pup has enough room to stand up, turn around, and lie down comfortably. However, there should not be enough room for your pup to use a corner as a potty spot. There are crates that you can get that are entirely adjustable—you will be able to change the sizes of the siding to accommodate your pup over time so you do not have to keep buying new ones.

- If your pup is going to be crated longer than an hour or two, you must ensure that there is a freshwater dispenser present for him or her to get fresh water whenever necessary.

- If you are not home during the potty-training period, make sure that you make arrangements for someone to come in and relieve your pup if you cannot get home. For example, if you work so you cannot get home every three or four hours, try asking a neighbor if they can keep an eye on your pup. You may be surprised to find that they are totally happy to do so.

- Discontinue this method if you find that your pup regularly relieves himself in the crate. You may have a crate that is too big and your pup is not learning.

Chapter Six: Training and Behavior Modification

Umbilical Training

Some people find that the best way they can train their Shiba Inu pup to avoid accidents is a method known as umbilical training. This is exactly what it sounds like—you will want to make sure that you tether yourself to your pup so your pup cannot get up and cause trouble elsewhere. You will primarily be doing this by using a leash. At first, you may find that this is inconvenient, but over time, you may come to realize that this is actually incredibly useful to you—you will be able to use this method to ensure that your pup is not out of your sight long enough to have an accident, and you will be able to respond to your pup immediately if you do see that he is getting ready to go.

When you do this, you will want to make the leash a decent length, but not long enough that your pup can slip away and out of sight. You will want to ensure that your pup is close enough that you can see him at all times. Beyond that, you simply keep your dog at your side. There is not much else to it beyond that—you just keep your pup with you as much as possible.

If your pup is resistant at first, don't give in. If he has had his freedom for a while, he may assume that he can, in fact, still be given free rein to wander as he wishes. However, that is not going to work for you—you need to be able to see him to immediately get him out. If you do find that he is starting to go outside only and accidents are no longer happening, then it could be time to let him have some more autonomy. However, any time that he starts to have accidents again, he will need to be tethered to you again.

Chapter Six: Training and Behavior Modification

Using a Bell at the Door

Some people like to train their pups to ring a doorbell when they need to go out. This allows them to sort of communicate or convey what it is that they need at any given moment. One of the best ways to do so is to get a strip of fabric or a thick rope and attach some bells to it. Then, place the bells on a hook next to the front door, low enough that your pup can reach them. Every time that you are going to go out with your pup to take him out, ring the bell. Over time, he will start to associate that sound of the bell ringing with you cuing to him that it is potty time. Over time, he will get better and better at this and he will be able to ring the bell himself when he needs to go.

The trick here, however, is that you have to believe him. If he rings the bell, you go outside to let him out. You will have to do it every time so he learns the message—he learns that if he rings the bell, he gets to go to his potty spot.

Teaching Your Puppy to Follow Commands

Ultimately, training your Shiba Inu puppy to follow commands is all about repetition and modeling. Over time, your pup will learn to begin to follow your commands. Training can be quite tricky to those that have never done it—pups do not inherently understand what you mean when you tell them to sit. It has to be learned over time and that can be quite tricky sometimes. We are going to go over the general process of training your pup in this chapter, going step by

Chapter Six: Training and Behavior Modification

step to see what you need to do and what your pup will likely do at each and every step along the way.

Timeline for Training Your Pup

Training your Shiba Inu pup can begin as soon as you have him home with you. While your pup is not going to have much in the way of an attention span yet, you are going to find that he is quite eager to please. During this juvenile stage, you are going to be teaching simple commands. You really are not working much more than teaching the rules of the house, what your pup can expect from you, and how you are going to interact with him or her. This is simple enough. This stage of training will be all about how you can interact with your pup in a gentle, positive manner and how likely you are to ensure that he or she is going to receive that message that you were trying to convey without a problem. This is more like encouraging your pup when they do happen to do what they want. You may be using treats to sort of guide the behavior, but you are not able to get them to truly understand it yet. This is like the foundation for the training that will come soon.

It is not until later, when your pup is around 6 months of age that he or she will be ready for proper, formal training. This is when you can start the processes of training all of the commands that you would really like to do. This is where you will be using the proper stages that will be introduced shortly and that you will be able to expect your dog to follow on a regular basis. These different steps that you will go through will be to introduce the command, reward the command when your pup gets it right, practice and reinforce the command, and then remembering to continue to train the command and use it regularly to ensure that it is not forgotten.

Introduce the Command

The first stage here is going to be introducing the command—you are going to be deciding which command that you want your pup to know and then stating that command out loud. Especially in the early days, then, you are going to facilitate getting the pup to move into the way that you are trying to get him to. If you want to, for example, train your pup to sit, you may say, "Sit." Immediately afterward, you then use a piece of food to entice your pup to shift into a proper sitting position. You would do this simply by moving the piece of food in front of him until he looks up at it, and then continue moving it behind him. You will sort of coerce him into flopping down on his bottom in a sitting position. You will want to make sure that you only state the command once when you are trying to get the pup to obey.

Reward the Command

As soon as the pup is in the right position, it is time to reinforce it—you do this through positively rewarding the pup for doing the right thing. You give him the food, praise him, and pet him. His mind has now connected the word that you said, the food, and the positive feelings all to that behavior that you are trying to train, and that is where the power is going to be coming from.

Chapter Six: Training and Behavior Modification

When you reward the command, you want to make sure that your pup is rewarded with something that is going to be desirable. Over time, however, you will begin to fade out the food as a reward for following through with the behavior. You may find that what works for you is a gesture along with the treat so the gesture gets paired in there, too. No matter what the command, however, you always want to make sure that you reward it, even when it is a basic one and your pup is fully grown. You can do this with a quick verbal affirmation and a pat on the head.

Practice the Command

Next comes practice. When it is time to practice those behaviors, you are putting the mall to good use and ensuring that the pup starts to connect the word that you are using to the action that you are asking for. This is done with patience and careful encouragement. Over time, however, you will find that your pup is quite eager to follow along. Your pup will be happy to give you the result you wanted if you are willing to reward him.

Practice will happen over a long period of time. Some commands may not take very much at all to reinforce but other more complex commands, such as trying to train a trick that has no real purpose other than entertainment, like playing dead in response to finger guns, will most likely take your pup much longer to figure out.

Reinforce the Command

Chapter Six: Training and Behavior Modification

Reinforcement will be an important step for you. Each and every time you find that your pup is doing what you have commanded, you must make sure that you reinforce it. You can do this with anything that you want to do. All that matters is that you are making sure that your pup is catching onto your expectations and that you are making sure that your pup is interested in continuing to follow them.

Continue Use of the Command

Finally, the last step to training your pup is ensuring that he is exposed to continued use of these commands as you continue to practice them. You want to ensure that your pup knows what you want. You also want to make sure that the automatic response between your command and the action will happen regularly without much of a problem. When you do this, you will find that you will actively be encouraging your pup to remember this command.

Every time you repeat the command in different contexts, you will find that you are encouraging him or her to continue to remember the command. You are strengthening that connection in your mind and in doing so, you will find that you will naturally get your pup to follow along with what you want.

When you first start training, you probably chose to do so in an environment that was not particularly distracting. It could have been at your home, for example, where there is not much going on. However, at some point, you will really need to reinforce that command by practicing it in a busier setting as well. You will need your pup to know to stop and listen to

Chapter Six: Training and Behavior Modification

you, no matter where you are or what you are doing, and because of that, you have to be able to train your pup under many different settings, reinforcing it as much as you can.

Basic Commands

Now that you know the difference between behavioral and obedience training you can approach both accordingly. You should already be establishing and maintaining boundaries, and it's now time to introduce some basic command drills.

It is worth mentioning again that you cannot simply practice commands a few times and then expect to move on to the next one. The following drills may look absurdly simple and you may be wondering where the rest of the information is but the truth is this is all you need.

Simplicity and consistency are the keys to learning so practice the below little and often to cement the knowledge long-term.

Tip: Before giving a command, call your dog's name to get his or her attention to ensure you have been heard.

Sit

This is the most common starting point and a great foundation for further obedience training. Here's how it's done:

Chapter Six: Training and Behavior Modification

1. Take a treat and let your dog see it, then hold it above his or her head. If they try to jump up remember to remind them of the boundaries you have set.

2. Now use your free hand to *gently* encourage their bottom to the ground and at the same time give a firm command of 'sit'.

3. Make sure he or she has obliged, and then give the treat as a reward. Be sure to offer verbal praise in the form of 'good boy' or 'good girl' every time too.

When your dog has the hang of sitting with assistance you can be gentler when pushing their bottom to the ground.

You can then progress to simply moving your hand towards their backside when giving the command – if they are learning then they will respond to this gesture and, eventually, will not need it at all.

As your dog gets older they will not need to be rewarded with a treat every time, but giving them one every so often is a fair reward for remembering commands.

Stay

Once your dog has learnt to sit without assistance it is ready to learn to stay put.

As you move away they are likely to want to follow you – don't encourage this behavior as it could become frustrating or even dangerous. For example, you don't want them under your feet in the kitchen or following you onto the street when you leave the house.

Chapter Six: Training and Behavior Modification

Here's how to have your dog stay rooted once they've sat down:

1. Start by having them sit and reward them for doing so.

2. Now hold your empty hands up in a 'stop' gesture and give the clear command 'stay'.

3. Back away a short distance and keep your hands up, repeating the command if necessary. If he or she gets up and follows you – which they probably will initially – say 'no' and lead them back to the sitting position to start the process all over again.

When your dog obeys this command, use the reward and praise techniques already learnt to ensure they know they've done well.

Down

Use this command to encourage your dog to lie on the ground. It's best to keep things simple here and avoid using the two word command 'lie down.'

Tip: Do not use 'down' as a disciplinary word when your dog jumps up at you or climbs on the furniture; this will become confusing when you train it to lie down later. Instead use 'off!' to combat this behavior.

1. Start with a treat half hidden in your hand and let your dog see it.

Chapter Six: Training and Behavior Modification

2. Give the 'sit' command but do not offer the treat immediately. Instead, lower your hand directly onto the ground and give the command 'down'.

3. The dog will likely scramble around your hand trying desperately to get at the treat, and this will normally lead them to get down on their belly. When they do this and have settled down, give them the treat and praise them for a job well done.

If your dog isn't lying down then you can give gentle assistance with your free hand, repeating the command just as you did during training to sit. You don't need to be forceful here – your dog is weaker than you and will only need a little encouragement.

Come

I'm sure you're starting to see the natural progression of these commands, just as your friend will if trained little and often.

Bear in mind that this particular command can be very confusing for a young dog that is just learning to sit and stay, so it is important not to cross command boundaries here. Let them get the hang of one thing before jumping to the next and do not overload them with different commands all at once.

Here's the drill:

1. Start with having the dog sit and stay, and reward them accordingly.

Chapter Six: Training and Behavior Modification

2. Back away as normal and allow a couple of moments to elapse so you are sure they have understood.

3. When they have sat calmly for 10 seconds, switch your stopping hand gesture to a welcoming and encouraging movement and give the command 'come!'

This should be all it takes to get them to come bounding over, but offer them a little extra encouragement if necessary. As with all successes, finish off with a reward.

4. Add the 'sit' command at the end of this drill as soon as possible to prevent jumping up.

Tip: avoid the temptation to meet your dog halfway – they must learn to do the work themselves. You can slowly increase the distance over time and eventually perform this command when out of eyeshot altogether, but take it slow at first and ensure the knowledge is sinking in.

Off

You may think your dog jumping up at you or other people is a show of affection, but that's not entirely true. Dogs can often be anxious and that causes them to bound towards people and seek comfort.

They jump up at you as a child would, seeking reassurance. By making a fuss, petting them or picking them up you will only encourage this behavior.

A puppy's mother would gently move them out of the way in order to create a clear boundary in cases such as this.

Chapter Six: Training and Behavior Modification

Here's a drill to replicate this yourself:

1. When you see your dog, do not give eye contact, speak to or physically come into contact with them until they are completely calm.

2. Once the dog is totally calm, try introducing the sit command if they are already familiar with it.

3. You may interact with your dog once you have clearly gained control of the situation.

Tip: teach your dog to sit whenever there is a knock at the door to prevent them racing up to visitors in the same way.

Drop

Your dog may occasionally latch onto things and not want to let go. Prevent this behavior with the following drill.

1. Offer your dog its favorite toy. You can even introduce the 'take it' command here to get them used to receiving things with permission.

2. Allow them to play for a while, and then have them sit in front of you with the toy.

3. Say 'drop' and at the same time offer a small food treat. Dogs always prefer food over fun so this should cause them to drop the toy.

Chapter Six: Training and Behavior Modification

Leave

Your dog's instincts will often take over, especially when it comes to food. Here's how to have them wait patiently for your approval.

1. Take a small food treat and place it in the palm of your hand, close to the gap between your thumb and index finger.

2. Close your fist and turn it over so the top of your hand is facing upwards.

3. Invite the dog to you and have it sit and sniff your hand. Once it finds the treat, state 'leave it' and wait for it to stop sniffing, nibbling or pawing momentarily and then open your hand to let them take the treat.

Tip: scale this drill up by asking your dog to 'leave it' as soon as you extend your hand towards them with the treat inside and making them wait longer to receive it. Eventually you will be able to begin this exercise with an open hand, or even with the treat on the floor.

Gently

If your dog has a habit of snatching you can prevent it by offering things in the correct manner. Use the below guidelines:

- Do not hold things in your fingertips as this makes it difficult for the dog to take.

Chapter Six: Training and Behavior Modification

- When your dog is comfortable with the 'leave' command and is sitting patiently waiting for a treat, introduce the 'gently' command to let them know they can take it. If they snatch, put your hand behind your back and state 'no!' before starting over.

Speak

Teaching your dog to bark on command can actually help prevent unwanted barking. It can also be useful for security purposes. Here's how:

1 Give your dog the 'speak' command and wait for him or her to bark two or three times.

2. Place a treat under their nose in a closed fist until they stop barking.

3. Once your dog has calmed down and is quiet, offer the treat.

Tip: Once your dog is taught to bark on demand, add the 'quiet' command before sticking the treat under his or her nose in order for them to make an association with the word.

Putting the Basics Together

Once your dog has mastered these techniques you can start putting them together. For example, when they have sat, have them stay. Once they've stayed put for a short time, have them come to you and then immediately command them to sit again.

Remember to keep the sessions short and productive and reward each success. If you become frustrated or the dog seems disinterested then call it quits and revisit the training a little later.

Separation Anxiety

It's important to understand separation anxiety because it should form a part of all puppy training.

Separation or canine separation anxiety can affect all dogs. Although research suggests that dogs are more likely to develop separation behavior problems if they are male, come from a shelter, or are separated from the litter before they are 60 days old.

Interestingly dogs born at home were more likely to suffer anxiety than those born with a breeder.

Dogs that tend to have higher levels of alertness, like Shiba Inus, are also thought to increase the chance of that dog experiencing separation anxiety.

In research, mixed breed dogs were more likely to destroy, urinate or defecate when left alone, whereas Wheaten Terriers were likely to vocalize, salivate or pant.

And where separation anxiety existed, almost all of the dogs also had a fear of noise. Miniature Schnauzers and Staffordshire Bull Terriers were the least affected by noise.

Chapter Six: Training and Behavior Modification

Not all dogs of the same breed will develop separation anxiety, it just means that there is a higher tendency that they might be more susceptible.

Shiba Inus are believed to be more likely to suffer from this due to their high levels of vigilance, energy and loyalty.

Causes and Signs Of Separation Anxiety

Separation anxiety is not a failure on the owner's part and there can be many reasons that a dog reacts like this.

There may have been a change in ownership either from another home or from a shelter, there may have been a house move or a change in the routine of the family, it might be due to divorce or the loss of a family member (usually another dog but it could be a cat or even a family member moving away to school).

For puppy's, it might simply be the first time they have been left alone having been used to being around people all the time.

Dogs may also have had a bad experience - firecrackers, a delivery person, or the noise from trash pick-up. Dogs don't like sudden and unexpected noises.

Like anyone, dogs can get more nervous if they are alone. But remember dogs are not used to dealing with threats alone, they are used to packs who are there for safety as well as nurture.

Chapter Six: Training and Behavior Modification

If they are already nervous or uncomfortable then they will feel even more vulnerable when they need to deal with these 'threats' alone in their home.

Finally, dogs may be bored. Boredom usually affects young or energetic dogs who still don't know what to do when they are left to play - or relax - alone and they will seek out ways to keep themselves entertained.

Like chewing furniture - this is also a calming activity - or exploring the trash. Exercise will help with this.

Dogs will do some of these things some of the time. But when they display this behavior some or most of the time then it is likely your dog is suffering from some degree of separation anxiety.

Dogs will get bored when they are left alone. Your dog will sleep – dogs sleep for between to 10 to 14 hours a day - but he will be awake at various points and he will be looking for something to do.

He might have a sniff around, have a drink or two, and then look for something else to occupy his mind, his energy, and his time.

Dogs like to put things in their mouth, some things fit in their mouths and some things don't. This means that sometimes the mess you discover on returning home is simply a sign of a bored dog and not necessarily one suffering from anxiety.

This doesn't make the experience of returning home any more pleasant but exercise will help and finding toys that

Chapter Six: Training and Behavior Modification

he can play with will relieve some of that boredom. Other signs, that are more likely to be separation anxiety, are more obvious.

Howling or barking is not the only sign of separation anxiety. Other signs are excessive barking, panting or whining, and indoor accidents. This won't be due to not being housebroken.

Stress can result in either peeing or pooping or both. They may also chew things to calm themselves, scratch at doors or windows and some might try to escape.

They are more likely to be scratching the door that you left from, or the window from where they can see you leave, they might chew something that smells of you - a shoe, sock, or even a magazine.

Signs of general stress in dogs will be panting and pacing and this may well be evident in your dog if he or she is suffering from separation anxiety.

Is your dog panting when you return home? This might be due to whining and barking while you were gone. You will notice this at other times too.

Separation anxiety is not only when you leave the house and the dog is alone. It can also be when dogs become anxious when they are not seated near you or can't see you even if you are still at home.

Does your dog follow you around and want to sit beside you all the time? Do they sit against your legs or feet

Chapter Six: Training and Behavior Modification

(this way they will know as soon as you move)? Again, Shiba Inus do like to follow you around.

What happens when you leave? Is it only you that your dog is focused on (if you share your home with family). In some cases, it doesn't matter if the dog is with another person in the home when you leave. Again, Shiba Inuss are often fixated on just one leader.

If you share your home and want to find this out, simply have a friend or another family member stay with your dog (with some treats) and leave the house.

How does your dog react? Do they ignore the treats and look for you and if they do, how long for? Or do they settle down with the other person and enjoy their treats?

If you are not sure how your dog is reacting when you leave then it is useful to record your dog when you are not there. What does he do when you leave? Does he go to the door for a few minutes - how long?

Take note of everything you can see and what he does. This is one of the best ways to find out what is happening when you are gone.

What To Watch Out For

Does your dog start to behave differently as you get ready to leave, either before you have started to get ready or when you are getting ready to leave?

Chapter Six: Training and Behavior Modification

The first thing to do is to take notice of their behavior and try and think about if it has changed and why it might have changed. What changes have you made, if any?

Notice how much and how often your dog is following you (even if he is a new puppy). If it's an older dog try to think back to any changes - is he sitting beside you more often, following your more than he used to? Is there any other reason or a point in time that you can identify?

The solution to this part of their behavior is to slowly build them up to being comfortable with you not being beside or near them so that they get used to your absence and learn (or re-learn) that you come back.

Sometimes any or some of the signs can be there for other reasons so if you are worried at all just check with your veterinary.

Why Punishment Won't Work

Before we talk about all the things that can be done to help with separation anxiety it is useful to understand why punishment just won't work.

Have you ever taken your dog over to the 'scene of the crime' and pointed at it. I have done this and we all will have done this.

Notice that the dog appears to look guilty and might cower. We, as humans, project our feelings or interpretation

Chapter Six: Training and Behavior Modification

onto this behavior and assume that the dog is noticing what it has done and feels 'guilty' about it.

This is not what is happening. What we see as 'looking guilty' is appeasement behavior. It can be a way that your dog is releasing tension to try and get rid of their fear. The cowering, flat ears and tail between the legs or looking away is your dog trying to placate you.

The dog will know that she emptied the trash all over the kitchen floor and dragged some of it into other rooms but it won't connect what it has done wrong.

And he definitely won't connect something that happened 2 or 3 hours ago when you arrive home to find the mess.

All your dog will know is that you are not happy and he will pick this up from you and be fearful and will try to placate you but he won't know what he has done.

Dogs won't associate something done hours or even minutes ago with the here-and-now. No matter how much we tell them, they simply won't understand why we are angry with them - just that we are.

And this means they won't understand why they are being punished. They will only connect that you arrive home and they get punished.

This means that punishment when you return home will make your dog not only stressed about you leaving, but stressed about you coming home too. This can make any anxiety worse.

Chapter Six: Training and Behavior Modification

Just remember, the dog has not done this to deliberately annoy you nor to 'get back' at you. He did it because he was stressed and anxious or bored and then tried to use that pent-up energy.

Preparation and Socialization

It's a good idea to get your puppy used to being separated from you when they are young. Even if you don't expect to be away from them often, there will be times when you will need to.

Teaching your puppy not to fear this absence and to let them know that they can be relaxed when you are not there is one of the best things you can do for both your puppy, and for yourself.

If your puppy can get used to being left for short periods when they are young then they are more likely to grow up feeling relaxed and comfortable when left on their own for part of the day.

These are all really simple things to do and are obvious once you know them. You will need to do this slowly, teaching them bit by bit over time.

The first 3 basic steps you need to take are the following ones.

1. Pick the room you want your puppy or dog to be in when you are not in the house - either in their basket, bed, or crate. Decide which room this is going to be as early as you can.

Chapter Six: Training and Behavior Modification

2. Once you decide on where this is, start getting them used to being in this room - don't wait until the time when you are going to leave the house.
3. Spend time with your puppy or dog in this room - you want them to understand it is not a punishment 'place' or a place that is apart from you but a part of their household.

Create a physical barrier between the room you want them to remain in and the room you are in - make this something they can see you through (like a gate).

Once you have picked the room that you want your dog to stay in when you leave the house, create a gate to the room but make it a barrier or gate so that your dog can still see you. Remember not to interact with your puppy or dog when they are there - just go about doing things as normal.

Don't forget to spend time with them in this room when you are not about to leave, spend time there during the day or when you are training them so that this becomes a place that you are a part of too.

As you begin their training, the first thing you will do after you have created the gate is to just be on the other side of the gate to your dog. Do this for 2 or 3 minutes but if your dog starts to get stressed just calmly let them out.

Keep building their confidence and slowly make the time longer. Start moving around and doing other things as you build up the time and distance. At this point, you will always be in sight.

Chapter Six: Training and Behavior Modification

If they start to get anxious just move forward or return to the point where they were comfortable. Once they are comfortable with the distance, start to move out of sight to another room for a few minutes and then repeat the process of stretching the time. Begin by moving to the door of the room.

Then move into another room out of sight (but they will still be able to hear and smell you). Return after a few minutes, and then repeat building up the time as you go along.

Finally, go to the main door and go outside for a few minutes. Once again repeat the process of increasing the time you are away and check how your dog is reacting.

If there are signs of stress or anxiety just go back a couple of steps and begin building up your dog's confidence once again. Keep the time as short as you need to, it can start with as little as 5 or 10 seconds and build the time based on your dog's response.

From the very start let the dog know that the place you have chosen is their safe place. Keep all their things in this room and place their bed or crate in here as soon as you can along with some toys.

If you are using a crate, keep the crate door open - let them get used to going in and out of the crate and choosing to do so.

Get some chew toys for them. Chew toys are good because chewing is calming action (and it's why they chew things they shouldn't). You could also put an item of your

Chapter Six: Training and Behavior Modification

clothing in the room so that they can more easily smell you and feel more secure.

The chew toys help your dog use their mind to try and work out how to get the food or treat removed. Giving a reason for dogs to exercise their mind keeps them busy and happily occupied.

A Kong is a great chew toy to use because, as well as the chewing, the fun of getting the treats or food out of the inside of the King exercises their mind.

Put on some sound - like a radio talk station. Not at a high volume - you only want to muffle any unexpected sounds. Whatever you choose make it something that you listen to so that they are familiar with it.

Your dog will be paying attention to any noise they hear so this can help disguise some of the day-to-day noises that might go on outside (or inside) your home. It is useful to do this as soon as you begin the training so that it becomes familiar.

Try to teach your dog not to follow you all the time in the home and get them to go to different places in the house. Test them being in a room while you are in another. Don't force this or make them feel stressed about it. You need to teach them to be comfortable with it.

Play a game where you ask them to remain in one room while you move to another, then come back. If they stay where they were, come back and give them a reward - it can be a treat or affection/well done. Once again, do this calmly because if you do, then you will keep your dog calm too.

Chapter Six: Training and Behavior Modification

Remember when you come back not to increase or cause excitement. This can be a great game for your dog and they will enjoy it as much as you enjoy the results of it.

When you are ready to start the next phase of actually leaving the house there a few more things you can do to keep your dog calm while you are out.

How To Leave And Return

Start by leaving the house for a minute, 2 minutes, 3 minutes, and so on and try and return before they are anxious. If you can, then leave for longer and build up to an hour and so on.

If you notice they are not comfortable, then go back to the point when they were, and start from there again. Build the time up again.

Aim to build the routine - perhaps a treat as you leave. But don't kiss and cuddle them and make a fuss with gestures and by your comments. Try and make it as normal and calm as possible.

Once you start leaving altogether, do so for short periods at the start, and build up the time to 2, 3 and 4 hours - and make sure they have something to play with or to eat.

Ideally, don't leave your dog alone for more than 4 hours. If you can ask a neighbor or a friend to visit - one your dog might know - or a dog walker. If you are able, come home from work for lunch.

Chapter Six: Training and Behavior Modification

You might start to notice that your dog starts to get anxious when you put on your shoes or coat or if you pick up keys or a bag.

If they start to react to these signs then start training them to get used to these things. Put on your shoes or coat or grab your keys but don't leave. Do something else or sit down and relax (or watch the TV). Keep doing this during the day so that they don't associate these things with your departure.

You can also try body-blocking. As soon as they started to get agitated as the boots or coat come out, interrupt his behavior by standing up straight and then asking him to go to his basket.

It's important not to be angry - they aren't doing anything wrong - you just want them to do something else so let them know what that is e.g. go to their crate or their basket.

You might need to re-trace your steps a few times and go back a few paces in the separation training from time-to-time as you are building their confidence and their sense of 'normal'. Just go back to the point where your dog was last comfortable.

Take this slowly - leave and come back. Build their knowledge and confidence. Having them exercised will help reduce their energy levels so remember to make sure they have had a walk and have been fed. This will make them tired.

You can also try giving them a favorite treat. This might help them associate your departure with something they can look forward to.

Chapter Six: Training and Behavior Modification

When you return, don't get them excited with happy cries of "Hello!". Don't over-excite them or over-reward them when you come back. Just arrive home and then ignore them for 5 minutes.

You need to make the exit and return a very normal thing rather than any kind of event to be excited about.

If they have done something wrong on your return don't punish them or shout at them. They won't understand why.

Summary

- Don't make a fuss of your dog when you leave. Don't and kiss them and say 'goodbye'.
- Leave calmly.
- Give them their favorite treat as you leave - give them something to chew on.
- Make sure they have been exercised.
- Don't excite them as soon as you return home, wait a few minutes before greeting them.

Leaving When Using A Crate

When you put your dog in their crate (if you use a crate) before you leave then don't close the door right away. Put them in and wait until they calm down or lie down.

This might take a few minutes or more so do something else and give them time to relax and be calm. Close and open the door a few times if you like but wait until they lie down before you close the door.

Chapter Six: Training and Behavior Modification

Don't bribe them into the crate with a treat and then immediately shut the door - just take your time and let them take their time to get comfortable.

Once they are comfortable in their space and their room then you can start moving away using the methods detailed in the first step.

Some Other Useful Tips

Exercise is an important part of curing separation anxiety and it is particularly important for Shiba Inus.

A 2015 study by PLoS One found that dogs with noise sensitivity and separation anxiety had less daily exercise.

This suggests that exercise is one of the biggest things you can do to prevent or improve separation anxiety in your dog.

You need to make sure your pet gets lots of exercise every day because a tired, happy dog will be less stressed when you leave.

The study also found that dogs that were exercised off-leash were less likely to suffer from separation anxiety or fear around noise. The likely reason for this is that being on a leash, partly on a leash, or running free has an impact on the amount of exercise a dog has.

A dog whines when it starts to get tense or excited - think of as them releasing their energy. Sometimes they whine because they want something - if this is the case, they will make it obvious what they want.

Chapter Six: Training and Behavior Modification

If you notice this and the reason is not obvious then try and work out why it might be excited and calm them down before the excitement level rises.

If you have multiple household members - try and share the dog equally amongst everyone - so the dog doesn't focus all their attention onto one person.

If there are more members then one can leave and he dog will worry less. Research shows that dogs in multiple person households are more likely to suffer from separation anxiety.

The 10 Steps To Help Separation Anxiety

1. Create a physical barrier between the room you want them to remain in and the room you are in - make this something they can see you through.
2. Put their bedding or basket in this room along with any of their toys and the bowls.
3. Put on some sound - like a radio talk station. Not at a high volume - you only want to muffle any unexpected sounds.
4. Teach your dog not to follow you all the time in the home.
5. Don't make a fuss of your dog when you leave. Don't cuddle and kiss them and say 'goodbye'
6. Leave calmly

Chapter Six: Training and Behavior Modification

7. Give them their favorite treat as you leave - give them something to chew on
8. Make sure they have been exercised
9. When you return don't over-excite your dog as soon as you arrive home (if there is a mess, don't punish your dog)
10. Wait a few minutes before you acknowledge them and say hello.

Common Behavior Problems

Once you are able to train your Shiba Inu a few of the commands, you will find that the puppy is going to behave the way that you would like. They will listen to the commands that you give and will get along with the family. However, each puppy is going to have a different kind of personality and it is possible that they will still deal with some problems that you will need to take care of.

Some puppies are not going to have any of these tough dog problems, and some are going to have a few that you need to deal with. Learning what your puppy is going to do when others come around, and what behaviors you need to fix and fixing them as quickly as possible, can be the key to having a puppy behave the way that you want. Some of the most common tough dog problems that your puppy may show and the steps you can take to deal with them include:

Chapter Six: Training and Behavior Modification

Jumping up on Other People

Do you find that your Shiba Inu likes to jump up on you and other people? For those who know what this is like, know that this is actually a behavior issue that should not be encouraged. Owners find that it can be hard to get dogs, no matter the age, to stop jumping up on them and some of the other people who are around them. Even if you don't feel like this is a big deal right now, think about how you are going to feel about the dog jumping on you or someone else when they are heavy? It is better to train your puppy to not jump on anyone from a young age. It is easier this way and ensures that they aren't going to be toppling other people over either.

First, we need to take a look at why the puppy is likely to jump on you or other people. For the most part, this is because they are excited. They see you or someone else come through the door and because they don't have the necessary self-control yet, and they want to jump up to show how excited they are to see you. Or, there may be times when the puppy is going to jump up because they see some item in your hand that they want, and they jump up to try and get it.

Either way, it is important to learn how to stop the Shiba Inu from jumping up on you and knocking you and others down. You need to remember to be consistent. You can't discourage the jumping one day and then be excited to see them another day and be fine with the jumping. Also, you can't have your cake and eat it too. You can't allow the dog to jump on you, and then train them not to jump on other people. This confuses the puppy and won't help you or them out at all. You have to decide that the jumping is a bad behavior, and then work to train them not to do it.

Chapter Six: Training and Behavior Modification

The good news here is that you are able to follow a simple process in order to get your puppy to listen to you and do what you would like. As with all of the unwanted behaviors that we are going to bring up in this chapter, you need to be strict about not allowing the puppy to jump on you ever. As you are going through the training process, and you see that the puppy is trying to jump on you, use the following steps to help prevent the behavior:

1. Tell the puppy, "OFF."
2. Turn your body around so that your puppy is looking directly at your back.
3. When you move the body so that it is turned around, the puppy is going to automatically get their paws back down on the floor and where they should be.
4. After the puppy has put their paws down, you can turn to face the puppy and then redirect them until they are sitting down.
5. Once the puppy listens and actually sits down, pet them, and reward them, showing the puppy that this is the way you want them to get your attention.
6. Now, there are going to be some times when the puppy will attempt to jump up on you again. If they start to do this, stop providing them with attention, and go through the steps above again. Only give the puppy some attention and affection when they are sitting down.
7. Practice with this each time that you come into the house, and even purposely leave for a few minutes

so that you get some more practice. Over time, this is going to become a habit, and the puppy will learn that they are not supposed to jump on you.

The point of doing this is to show the puppy that they are only going to get attention when they sit, rather than getting any attention when they are up and moving and jumping on others. This will help stop them from jumping on you and can do some wonders for teaching them some self-control along the way.

Destructive Chewing

Another issue that a lot of puppies will fall into is that they will start to chew on a lot of things that they shouldn't, many items that you do not allow, and are not part of their chew toys. When you first bring a Shiba Inu puppy home, especially if they are only about eight weeks old, remember that they don't know what is and what is not allowed to chew on. You have to step up and teach them these rules. Sure, it is easy to get frustrated with the puppy when they chew on the wrong thing, but you have to be proactive and teach your puppy what is appropriate behavior, especially when it comes to chewing.

While it may feel like the puppy is purposely being naughty and just had to go after your favorite pair of shews, remember that there are a lot of reasons why the puppy is chewing in the first place. They aren't trying to be naughty, and they aren't trying to make life more difficult for you. Some of the reasons that your puppy may be chewing on things include:

Chapter Six: Training and Behavior Modification

1. Dogs have a need that is instinctual that tells them to chew on things.
2. Chewing is a good outlet for most puppies when it is time to exert energy. Your dog could be chewing on a variety of items when they have a lot of energy that they need to get rid of, or when they feel a bit bored with their activities.
3. Similar to what we see with infants, puppies like to put objects into their mouths in the hopes of figuring out what the object is, and what they should do with it.
4. Puppies will often chew when they are teething. This chewing method is going to be a good way for them to soothe their gums.

Your dog is going to chew, and they need to chew, no matter if they are a brand new puppy or you have had them around for some time. You can't stop them from chewing, but you can control what they are allowed to do this with. You just need to pick out the right chew toys or items that you are going to give to the puppy and teach them what they can chew on, and what they need to avoid.

The good news is there are a few things that you are able to do in order to make sure the puppy is going to chew on the right items, and that they won't start to chew on some of your favorite items or on anything that they shouldn't have their mouths on. Some of the rules that you are able to follow when it comes to this include:

1. Always have some approved chewing objects that you can give to your puppy. Your puppy is going to chew no matter what, so make sure that you

Chapter Six: Training and Behavior Modification

provide them with some toys or objects that they are allowed to chew on instead of getting mad when they chew on items that you don't approve of.

2. Be strict with what they can chew on, and what they can't chew on. In the beginning, you have to be strict on this and may have to keep the puppy confined to one area. But this is their learning period, and you are going to see the best results when you can keep track of the puppy and make sure that they don't get ahold of things they shouldn't have.

3. Redirect the puppy to an object that you approve of for them to chew on. The puppy is sometimes going to get away from you and will try to chew on something that they should not. When you catch them in the act, don't try to shout or yell or get mad about it. This just encourages them because the puppy sees that they are getting attention from this. Instead, when you find them, say "NO" and then redirect them over to an item that is designed for them to chew on.

Pulling on the Leash

Another common issue that you will see when you bring home a new Shiba Inu puppy is that they like to pull on the leash. This one seems to be a really hard problem for most dog owners to deal with, and it seems like most owners are going to allow their puppy to pull on the leash forever. The good news is that it is possible to train your puppy to stop pulling on the leash, making things a whole lot easier for you.

Chapter Six: Training and Behavior Modification

The bottom line to remember here is that your leash should never be tight when you try to take the puppy on a walk. A loose leash is going to be the standard that you set, and it means that there is a little bit of slack on the leash between the puppy and you. There are a few reasons why you would want this to happen. It is going to teach the puppy that you are the pack leader and they should respect you. You don't want the puppy to start to think that they get to lead you all the time. When the puppy decides to make the leash tight and pulls on it, it is going to add a ton of stress and pressure to the neck, and this can be harmful to them. Pulling can also cause some damage to your own joints on the shoulders and arms. And when the puppy goes with a loose leash, it is going to become a much more enjoyable walk for both of you.

Now, this brings up the question of what you are supposed to do when the puppy decides to pull on the leash when you are walking. This may slow down your walk a bit, but you will find that most puppies are going to catch on quick, and doing this can really make a difference in how well the walk goes. Taking some time now will help you have much more pleasant walks overall. Some of the steps that you are able to do to help stop the puppy from pulling on the leash will include:

1. Any time that you feel the dog is getting excited and starts pulling on the leash, stop right where you are and don't go any further.
2. When the puppy starts to see that you have stopped and looks back at you, work with the clicker word.

Chapter Six: Training and Behavior Modification

3. Wait for the puppy to walk back to you, and when the puppy does this, reward them with a treat.
4. If you notice that the puppy is not coming back to you, lure them back using the heeling position and with a treat if you need it.
5. Now, there are some times when the puppy is still not going to come over to you. If this is the case, you can take another step back. Continue to do this until the puppy starts to walk back to you.
6. Repeat this process as many times as you need during the walk until the puppy learns that the leash needs to be loose.

As you can imagine, this is going to slow down the walk for a bit. You may only want to go on a walk down the block or so until the puppy starts to get the hang of what you are doing. The good news here is that the puppy will learn, and you will get the puppy to walk alongside you, with a nice loose leash rather than one that is tight and harming both you and the puppy, in no time.

The Puppy Doesn't Want to Walk on the Leash

There are some puppies who are so excited to go on a walk that they will bounce around, and then, once you are outside, they are going to pull on the leash, and you need to work on that problem. But then there are the puppies that don't like to walk on the leash at all. This is common for puppies who haven't been exposed to the leash at all. Most of the time they are going to catch on pretty quickly though, you just need to do a few steps in order to make this work for you. Some of the steps that you can use to get your Shiba Inu

Chapter Six: Training and Behavior Modification

puppy more used to the leash and doing what you want with it include:

1. Pull on the leash a bit, gently to the side while telling the command of "come" to the puppy.
2. If you find that this is not working, then call the puppy to you with a treat or something else that can be a reward.
3. If neither of the two steps above are working, you can try it with a harness and just repeat the steps that we have from above. You will find that the harness can be a nice addition because it gives you a bit more control over the puppy while making it so that you don't put too much pressure on the neck of your puppy.
4. Once the puppy listens to you and walks over, reward the puppy with a treat and a clicker word.
5. If you find that the puppy is responding pretty well with this, try calling the puppy to you without the treat, and use the clicker word on its own as a reward.
6. Repeat the process again until your puppy gets more familiar with the leash and doesn't seem to mind it as much.

Too Much Roughhousing with the Puppy

You will find that in some instances, your puppy is going to get into a really crazy mood where they will zoom around so much that they end up losing their self-control and won't behave well. When a puppy is in this kind of state, you

Chapter Six: Training and Behavior Modification

will find that redirecting the puppy is not going to be enough. The more excitement that the puppy has, the harder it is to get the puppy to control themselves. This means that you need to step up and gain control before the puppy has their energy escalate too high.

This is going to require the whole family getting on board and making sure they are all on the same page. If the kids are working to rile the puppy up, it could get out of control before you even have a chance to slow it down a bit. The sooner you are able to slow the puppy down; the easier things are going to be for you.

What this means is if you see that the excitement of the puppy is starting to build, it is time to gain control right away. You can have them sit or do one of the other commands that gets them to stop and listen to you. Sitting is a good way to force the puppy to have some self-control and calm down.

Now, there may be some times when the puppy is going to be in this state already. This means that the puppy is going to have already lost their self-control, and you and the rest of the family may need to remove yourselves from the situation so that they don't exert this loss of control onto the kids or you at this time. Another option that can work with this is to put the dog in the leash and take them outside to wear out some of that energy or let them run in the backyard. This helps to get some of that pent up energy out, and then the puppy will be able to exert the self-control again.

Chapter Six: Training and Behavior Modification

Fearfulness

There are some puppies who are going to be more reserved and may have some fears of the world, or at least a fear of things that are unfamiliar. It is natural to want to shelter them from the things that they fear, but this actually is going to cause the puppy more harm than good. The key in cases of fearfulness is to try and expose the puppy to the things that they are afraid of, but you should do it in a positive, as well as in a gradual, manner.

If you notice that you have a puppy that seems to be afraid of trying out anything new, or they have some fears that they can't seem to get over, there are a few steps that you can try out including:

1. Give your puppy some exposure to the thing that they are afraid of. Do this in a very slow manner so that they have time to look it over and explore it.
2. Start out with a big distance between the object the puppy is scared of and the puppy itself.
3. Associate the object of the puppy's fear with a lot of positivity. A good way to do this is to add something that the puppy really likes or really loves into that situation.
4. If your puppy is motivated by food, make sure that they are given a lot of treats while you expose them to that object.
5. Slowly start to move the puppy a bit closer to the object that they are scared about. Let them have some time to gain comfort with each distance to the object. Keep in mind that slowly is going to vary based on the puppy and how they are

Chapter Six: Training and Behavior Modification

reacting to this process. You have to go at the speed and the distance that works the best for your puppy.
6. If you find that the puppy seems pretty comfortable and unstressed, you may be able to approach the object of their fear on that same day. But for some puppies, moving them just a bit closer each day is going to be the best option.

You will need to repeat this process again and again, going a bit closer each day, until the puppy has been able to overcome their fears. Throughout the whole process, make sure to pay attention to the body language of the puppy, and learn their signals. You do not want to have them become too stressed out, and you don't want to push the puppy past their limits because this is just going to make things worse, and the puppy will start to fear the object more than before.

The Escape Artist

Hopefully you are able to read this part of the guidebook before the puppy has been able to escape out of your home and run away. Obviously, having the puppy escape and get lost is a traumatic experience for the whole family. But if the puppy is able to do this once, then it is likely they will continue to do this again and again.

There are several reasons why the puppy is going to try and get out of the home. They are allowed to roam freely, get into things, and do anything that they want. When they are out of the home, and away from you, they don't have to

Chapter Six: Training and Behavior Modification

follow any of the rules any longer! Escaping is going to be a kind of self-rewarding behavior for a dog, and because of this fact, it is going to be a hard one to break if the puppy has already been able to do this.

This means that your goal needs to be to prevent the puppy from getting out and escaping from the home in the first place. Some of the steps that you can take to help prevent your dog from bolting or escaping from your home will include:

1. Make sure that you are fully aware of where your dog is each time that you are about to go out the door. Make sure that all of the people in the home, even visitors, are aware of this kind of rule.
2. Train your dog to sit and consistently wait before going outside can be useful for this, as well. It may take a bit more time and patience, and it is likely that the dog won't want to do it, but it helps them to know they have to sit still if they want to go out.
3. If your back yard has a fence, then you need to make sure that it is secure in every place. You do not want to have any places on the fence or in the yard where your puppy will be able to get through.
4. If you do not have a fenced in back yard, then you need to make sure that the puppy is always on a leash.

The last point that is up above is going to be important. You may be tempted to keep the puppy off the leash because they have been behaving and have not been getting off the leash lately. But this gives the puppy a perfect chance to

Chapter Six: Training and Behavior Modification

escape. You have to be consistent with this so that the puppy will know their boundaries.

Too Much Whining and Barking

You will find that an excessive amount of barking is going to be a really frustrating behavioral issue that you, as a new owner of a Shiba Inu puppy, will have to deal with. This is also one of the biggest stressors that come up with a dog and their owner. This is why it is so important to solve the problem before it gets to a level that is too hard to control.

First, you need to be able to understand why the puppy is barking so much in the first place. Some of the reasons why your puppy may be barking so much to start with will include:

1. To try and get your attention
2. Because they are uncertain or fearful about something.
3. They want to be able to assert their own dominance over a passerby or another animal.

There are different steps that you will need to take based on what the puppy is barking at. If you find that the puppy is barking at you at this time, then it is because they want to gain more control, or they want your attention. Whether your puppy wants to be with the rest of the pack or they need some more exercise or something else, this is a behavior that you need to correct right away. The steps that you can take to make this work include:

1. If you notice that the puppy continues to bark, turn your back to them and continue to ignore them until they stop.

Chapter Six: Training and Behavior Modification

2. Have some patience here because the puppy is going to continue their barking, in some cases, for a long period of time.
3. Once the puppy does stop barking, no matter how long it took, you can turn around and give the puppy lots of praise, treats, and attention.
4. Any time that the puppy starts to bark at you, repeat this process until they stop barking. This lets them know that you will only give them attention if they are not barking.
5. If you can't get the puppy to stop barking, then it is time to take a break in the crate until they are all done.

In some cases, the puppy is going to bark at passerby and animals. This issue is sometimes embarrassing when you bring your puppy in public, but some people may feel a bit frightened if they don't know your dog. Many times, the owner is going to reinforce this behavior by screaming at the puppy to stop. You need to shift up the way that you respond to the barking first to get them to listen.

Let's say that the puppy is barking when they look at people or dogs through the window. Some of the steps that you are able to use in order to get the puppy to stop barking in this manner include:

1. Call the puppy's name in a positive manner so that they put their focus on you instead of the object of their attention outside.
2. The positive aspect of this is going to be the most important thing that you can do, but it is often the hardest as well. You need to find a way to be more

Chapter Six: Training and Behavior Modification

motivating to the puppy than what they see outside.

3. Once the puppy does look over at you, reward them before refocusing their attention on something else that they like, such as a bone or a toy, so they don't get distracted again and start barking.

It is also possible that your puppy is going to start barking at some people and other animals when they are in public. You are not going to be able to demand that they listen to you in the same manner that you could when at home. But this also doesn't mean that you have to just let the puppy bark all day long while you are out in public, or that you have to go home. When you have a puppy who is barking at people and other animals when they are out in public, some of the steps that you can take include:

1. If you have a puppy who is already barking, it is time to move far enough away from the focus of their bark so that they stop the barking. If you are aware of a stimulus that may cause the puppy to bark, try to start out far enough away so that they aren't going to bark at it to start with.
2. When the puppy is looking in the direction of the stimuli, call their name and do what it takes to redirect their focus back on you. When the puppy looks at you, give them a treat. This is going to help them to associate that stimulus with positivity.
3. As you get the puppy to self-control and calm down, see if you are able to move a bit closer to the stimuli. With each step, stop and redirect the

Chapter Six: Training and Behavior Modification

puppy back to you, and get them to gain the self-control that you want. The degree you move is going to vary between each animal, so take your time and see what works for your dog.
4. During this process, make sure that you are the one who is maintaining the control, not the dog. Check on a regular basis that the puppy remains relaxed during this process.
5. If you move closer and your puppy starts to bark again, it is time to move further away and then work to focus their attention back onto you before trying again.

Being on the Furniture

If you do not want the Shiba Inu to get up on your furniture, then this is another problem that you will need to work on as soon as possible. Remember that this one is up to you. Some people don't mind the puppy being on the furniture, and some don't want the puppy there at all. Either one is fine as long as you are consistent all the way.

For those who don't want their puppy on the furniture for one reason or another, this is just fine, but you need to start early, be firm with your decision, and be consistent. It isn't going to work if you sometimes allow the puppy on the furniture, and then other times, they are not allowed up there. It also will not work if you tell the puppy not to get on the furniture, but then others in the family allow the puppy to get up there.

If you have decided that you do not want to have your puppy to be up on the furniture, some of the steps that you

Chapter Six: Training and Behavior Modification

are going to take in order to make sure that the puppy will stay off your furniture include:

1. Be strict right from the start and make sure that the puppy is never allowed on the furniture.
2. Any time that the puppy tries to jump up on the furniture, tell them "OFF."
3. Motivate the puppy to get off of your furniture and back to the floor by drawing them down with a treat or a toy. If you find that the puppy is not really willing to get off the furniture with this, then it is fine to guide the puppy down with the use of their collar to follow your No.
4. Make sure to reward the puppy with praise, a treat, and the clicker word when they do get off the furniture. Remember, with this one that prevention is going to be the best way to work through the behavior, and if you find that the puppy is heading for the couch, be ahead of the game and automatically direct them to sit and give them a reward in the process.

Digging

While this is not really a behavior that is going to be bad for the puppy, it can be harmful to your yard, and this may be the reason that you stop it. Of course, most people don't want to look out in their yard and see a bunch of holes everywhere, so dealing with this problem right from the start can really help.

The first thing that we need to look at here is some of the reasons that a dog is going to dig. Each dog will be a bit

Chapter Six: Training and Behavior Modification

different, but generally, a dog is going to dig because their breed has a genetic disposition to digging, they are using this to help them get their energy out, or they feel bored.

This is one of those times when it is best to be preventative to make sure the puppy does not dig. Exercising and stimulating your puppy can help them to not get bored, and it gets all of that extra energy out so that they are not likely to dig in your yard any longer. A puppy who is exerting all of their energy with playing with their toys, chewing on bones, and getting out on walks is going to find that they have no need to go to the yard and dig some holes. If genetics are the problem, then there probably isn't much that you can do preventatively with this one. You just need to learn how to correct the behavior to get it to stop with your puppy.

If you do happen to catch the dog digging in your yard and you want to get them to stop, there are a few steps that you are able to take. Some of these steps include:

1. If you find that your dog is already digging in your yard, tell them "NO" in a firm manner and get them away and distracted from the hole.
   If you can, immediately redirect him to an appropriate item he can exert his energy into, such as running around the yard or chewing on a bone.
2. If you find a new hole that you didn't catch your puppy digging, there is nothing that you should do about the behavior. You need to make sure that you catch them in the act. If it is after the fact, then you are out of luck.

Chapter Six: Training and Behavior Modification

Remember that you are not able to discipline the puppy for something they did that you weren't able to catch them doing.

Your puppy is not going to remember that they dug the hole, even if it was just a minute ago. Scolding the puppy later on, is not going to do you any good because the puppy won't have any idea what you are scolding them for.

As you can see, there are a lot of behaviors that your puppy may show off that are going to make life a bit harder when you are working with your puppy. It is best if you are able to be proactive with this process and learn how to deal with the behaviors before they get even worse. The sooner that you are able to deal with these problems, the easier it is going to be. Following the steps that are in this chapter will make it easier for you to really get your puppy to behave in the manner that you would like.

Chapter Six: Training and Behavior Modification

Chapter Seven: Vet Care for Your Shiba Inu

Shiba Inus are considered to be a generally healthy breed. That being said, some diseases affect the Shiba Inu and it is important to make sure that you purchase a dog from a reputable breeder.

By purchasing from a breeder who health tests his or her lines, you are less likely to run into the hereditary illnesses that can affect the breed.

Note: Breeders who have long-standing bloodlines and have several generations of those bloodlines will often no longer test generations as if they are cleared for those diseases they cannot be passed to the next generation. This is not true. Some diseases can still crop up, even if parents and grandparents have not had a disease. On the other hand, it is probably not necessary to test dogs for every possible disease that can occur in a breed if the disease is extremely rare.

Signs of Illness

Although signs of illness may differ depending on the disease or illness affecting a dog, there are some general signs that you should look out for.

When your Shiba Inu has any of these symptoms, it is important to seek veterinarian care.

One thing that must be stressed with any breed, including the Shiba Inu, is that often illnesses are sudden, and it is very easy for a dog to go from healthy to gravely ill. Make sure you monitor your Shiba Inu frequently and carry out a daily health check.

Symptoms that your dog may be sick are:

Bad Breath

Bad breath is often a sign of some oral problem, but it can also be a sign of other diseases. If your dog has bad breath, and there is no root cause for it that you can see, schedule an appointment with your vet.

Drooling

Shiba Inus can drool at times, but excess drooling is a tip-off that there could be a health problem. If your dog is

Chapter Seven: Vet Care for Your Shiba Inu

drooling a lot, make an appointment to see your vet right away.

Loss of Appetite

Loss of appetite is often one of the first indicators that something is wrong with your Shiba Inu. With the loss of appetite, it is very important to look at the pattern of eating. If your dog is usually a picky eater, missing the occasional meal should not give rise to concerns.

Excessive Thirst

Outside of days with hot weather, if your Shiba Inu seems to be drinking large amounts of water, then it could be an indication of disease or dehydration. In general, an Shiba Inu should drink about an ounce of water for every pound of dog.

Changes in Urination

Changes in the color of urine as well as the frequency of urination can indicate a health problem. It is important to note that an increase in urination can be linked to some illnesses while difficulty urinating can indicate other problems. If you spot blood in the urine, contact your vet immediately.

Skin Problems

If your dog's skin is a bright red or you see flaking skin, then it could be a problem with your dog's health.

Besides, if the dog is itching a lot, it could have fleas, some type of mite or the dog could also have allergies. Make sure you check off all the reasons for the skin problems.

Lethargy

Shiba Inus are usually active dogs, but they do rest and sleep at times. However, lethargy is not normal. Like changes in appetite, make sure that you identify any reasons why your dog is tired, such as being over-exercised. If there are no apparent reasons, contact your vet.

Common Diseases/Illnesses

Hip Dysplasia: This is a heritable situation wherein the femur would not match snugly into the pelvic socket of the hip joint. Hip dysplasia can exist with or without medical signs. Some dogs exhibit pain and lameness on one or each rear legs. As the dog ages, arthritis can develop. X-ray screening for hip dysplasia is executed by means of the Orthopedic Foundation for Animals or the University of Pennsylvania Hip Improvement Program. Dogs with hip dysplasia ought to no longer be bred. Ask the breeder for evidence that the mother and father have been tested for hip dysplasia and found to be free of troubles.

Chapter Seven: Vet Care for Your Shiba Inu

Elbow Dysplasia: This is a heritable circumstance common to massive-breed puppies. It's idea to be due to specific growth rates of the three bones that make up the canine's elbow, causing joint laxity. This can result in painful lameness. Your vet may suggest surgical treatment to correct the problem, or medicine to govern the ache.

Epilepsy: The Shiba Inu can suffer from epilepsy, that's a sickness that reasons seizures. Epilepsy can be handled with medication, but it cannot be cured. A canine can stay a full and healthful existence with the right control of this hereditary disorder.

Deafness: Deafness within reason common in this breed and may pose many challenges. Some types of deafness and listening to loss may be handled with remedy and surgery, however commonly deafness cannot be cured. Living with and schooling a deaf dog calls for persistence and time, however there are many aids on the market, including vibrating collars, to make existence less difficult. If your Shiba Inu is identified with hearing loss or general deafness, take the time to assess if you have the patience, time, and capability to take care of the animal. Regardless of your selection, it is satisfactory to inform the breeder. '

Osteochondrosis Dissecans (OCD): This orthopedic situation, as a result of unsuitable boom of cartilage in the joints, generally occurs inside the elbows, but it's been seen within the shoulders as well. It reasons a painful stiffening of the joint, to the factor that the dog is unable to bend his elbow. It may be detected in puppies as early as four to nine months of age. Overfeeding of "increase formula" puppy meals or excessive-protein ingredients may make contributions to its improvement.

Progressive Retinal Atrophy (PRA): This is a degenerative eye ailment that in the end reasons blindness from the loss of photoreceptors in the back of the eye. PRA is detectable years earlier than the dog indicates any symptoms of blindness. Fortunately, puppies can use their other senses to atone for blindness, and a blind canine can live a full and satisfied life. Just don't make it a habit to move the furnishings round. Reputable Shiba Inu breeders have their puppies' eyes licensed annually by using a veterinary ophthalmologist and do not breed puppies with this disease.

Cataracts: A cataract is an opacity at the lens of the eye that reasons problem in seeing. The eye(s) of the dog may have a cloudy look. Cataracts commonly occur in vintage age and once in a while may be surgically eliminated to improve the canine's imaginative and prescient.

Distichiasis: This situation occurs whilst an additional row of eyelashes (referred to as distichia) grow on the oil gland within the dog's eye and protrude along the brink of the eyelid. This irritates the attention, and you could word your Shiba Inu squinting or rubbing his eye(s). Distichiasis is dealt with surgically by means of freezing the extra eyelashes with liquid nitrogen after which take away them. This kind of surgical procedure is known as cryoepilation and is completed underneath popular anesthesia.

Collie Eye Anomaly (CEA): Collie Eye Anomaly is an inherited circumstance that can result in blindness in some dogs. It generally takes place by the point the canine is 2 years

Chapter Seven: Vet Care for Your Shiba Inu

old and is recognized by a veterinary ophthalmologist. There is no treatment for CEA, but as noted above, blind dogs can get around thoroughly the use of their different senses. It is critical to remember the fact that this condition is a genetic abnormality, and your breeder ought to be notified if your pup has the condition. It is also essential to spay or neuter your dog to prevent the gene from being passed to a new generation of dogs.

Persistent Pupillary Membranes (PPM): Persistent Pupillary Membranes are strands of tissue in the eye, remnants of the fetal membrane that nourished the lenses of the eyes earlier than start. They usually disappear by the point a domestic dog is 4 or 5 weeks antique, but once in a while they persist. The strands can stretch from iris to iris, iris to lens, or cornea to iris, and from time to time they may be observed inside the anterior (front) chamber of the eye. For many puppies, the strands do not cause any issues and generally they smash down with the aid of 8 weeks of age. If the strands do no longer ruin down, they could cause cataracts or reason corneal opacities. Eye drops prescribed with the aid of your veterinarian can help spoil them down.

Hypothyroidism: Hypothyroidism is an abnormally low degree of the hormone produced by way of the thyroid gland. A mild sign of the disease may be infertility. More obvious signs include obesity, mental dullness, and lethargy, drooping of the eyelids, low energy degrees, and abnormal warmness cycles.

The canine's fur becomes coarse and brittle and starts off evolved to fall out, even as the skin will become tough and dark. Hypothyroidism can be handled with day by day medicinal drug, which should continue for the duration of the dog's life. A canine receiving every day thyroid remedy can live a full and satisfied existence.

Allergies: Allergies are a commonplace ailment in puppies. Allergies to positive meals are identified and handled by putting off sure meals from the canine's food plan until the offender is determined. Contact allergic reactions are resulting from a reaction to something that touches the dog, which includes bedding, flea powders, canine shampoos, or other chemical compounds. They are dealt with via identifying and removing the cause of the hypersensitive reaction. Inhalant hypersensitive reactions are caused by airborne allergens together with pollen, dust, and mildew. The appropriate medication for inhalant allergies depends at the severity of the allergy. Ear infections are a commonplace aspect impact of inhalant allergies.

Drug Sensitivity: Sensitivity to certain pills is generally seen in some breeds. It is as a result of a mutation of the Multidrug Resistance Gene (MDR1), which produces a protein referred to as P-glycoprotein. This protein works as a pump to put off poisonous substances from the frame to prevent the harmful effects of the toxins. In puppies who display Drug Sensitivity, that gene does not characteristic, resulting in toxicity. Dogs with this mutated gene may be touchy to ivermectin, a remedy generally used in anti-parasitic products along with heartworm preventives, as well as different capsules, including chemotherapy pills. Signs of this sensitivity range from tremors, depression, seizures, in-coordination, hyper salivation, coma, and even death. There

Chapter Seven: Vet Care for Your Shiba Inu

isn't any recognized remedy however there is a new genetic check that could pick out dogs with this nonfunctioning gene. All Shiba Inus must be screened.

Cancer: Dogs, like humans, can expand most cancers. There are many specific sorts of most cancers and the success of remedy differs for every person case. For some varieties of most cancers, the tumors are surgically removed, others are treated with chemotherapy, and a few are treated both surgically and medically.

Nasal Solar Dermatitis: Also referred to as Collie-nostril, this circumstance normally takes place in dogs who've little or no pigment in their nostril and isn't always restrained to Collies. Dogs who are exquisite-sensitive to daylight expand lesions at the nostril and from time to time around the eyelids, ranging from light red lesions to ulcerating lesions. The condition may be difficult to diagnose at first due to the fact several different illnesses can purpose the same lesions. If your Shiba Inu is recognized with Collie nose, preserve him out of direct daylight, and practice doggie sunscreen when he is going out of doors. The handiest way to control the circumstance is to tattoo the canine's nostril black so the ink serves as a protect against sunlight.

Detached Retina: A damage to the face can reason the retina to become indifferent from its underlying supportive tissues. A detached retina can result in visible impairment or maybe blindness. There isn't any treatment for a detached retina, however many dogs stay complete lives with visual impairments.

Chapter Seven: Vet Care for Your Shiba Inu

Finding a Good Vet

As a dog owner, searching for a good veterinarian is a kind of decision you mustn't take lightly. Surely, an outstanding pet health care provider can help you provide the best care to your dog. Pet owners certainly wish to be ensured that the veterinarian they choose will provide their pet the most superior standard of care probable. Not to mention, they prefer a vet who is more than willing to get in touch with them and educate them on how to manage and take proper care of their dogs.

If your Shiba Inu is not physically healthy, he or she will not be a happy canine companion for very long, because suffering from health-related issues can easily create a miserable and ill-mannered dog.

It's prudent that you take the many steps outlined here to help ensure that you are doing all that you can to keep on top of your Shiba Inu's good health.

Make sure you take the time to choose a veterinarian that can provide yearly check-ups, have your dog spayed or neutered in a timely fashion, choose a healthy diet for him or her, and carefully read this section so that you educate yourself about issues that may adversely affect your dog's health.

As well, take the time to learn a little canine CPR, because doing so may save the life of your dog, or someone else's.

Chapter Seven: Vet Care for Your Shiba Inu

Some clinics specialize in caring for smaller pets, while some specialize in larger animal care, and others have a wide-ranging area of expertise and will care for all animals, including livestock and reptiles.

Choosing a good veterinary clinic will be very similar to choosing the right health care clinic or doctor for your health because you want to ensure that your puppy or adult dog receives the quality care they deserve. A good place to begin your search will be by asking other dog owners where they take their furry friends and whether they are happy with the service they receive.

Take your Shiba Inu into your chosen clinic several times before they need to be there for any treatment so that they are not fearful of the new smells and unfamiliar surroundings.

Vaccinations

Most breeders will advise you to take your new puppy to the vet within 48 to 72 hours after bringing him home. This is good for everyone involved: you, the breeder, and the puppy. If you have a contract with the breeder, it probably has this kind of stipulation in it. It is important to make sure that the puppy is in good health when he arrives at your home. Depending on his age and where he is in his vaccination schedule, you may also be able to get his next vaccinations when you visit the vet for this check-up.

Chapter Seven: Vet Care for Your Shiba Inu

Recommended vaccinations can vary slightly, depending on where you live. Standard puppy vaccinations in Great Britain include the following:

a) Canine Parvovirus
b) Canine Distemper
c) Canine Parainfluenza Virus
d) Infectious Canine Hepatitis
e) Kennel Cough
f) Leptospirosis

Rabies is usually only given to dogs in the UK if they are planning a trip abroad since rabies has been eradicated in Great Britain.

Puppies receive the same vaccinations in the United States, though Leptospirosis is considered optional, depending on where you live. In some areas, a vaccination for Lyme disease (spread by ticks) can also be given, but it is not considered a basic vaccination. The rabies vaccine, however, is required for dogs by every state, usually by the time a puppy is four months old.

Some of these vaccines, such as the parvo vaccine, need to be given several times for several weeks to make sure the puppy is fully immunized. Once your puppy's vaccinations are completed, he will need to have booster shots when he is a year old. After that, the vaccines will need to be updated every two to three years, so your puppy won't need to get all of the vaccinations at the same time again.

Chapter Seven: Vet Care for Your Shiba Inu

Educate Yourself About Common Canine Diseases and Viruses

While your dog may never suffer from a common disease or virus, to ensure the safety and health of your happy Shiba Inu, you need to be aware of the many common diseases and viruses that could detrimentally affect the health of your dog.

Always watch out for the symptoms of the following common diseases and if you suspect that your dog has been infected, contact your vet immediately.

Be Aware That Allergies Can Adversely Affect Your Dog's Health

You may be surprised to learn that dogs can suffer from allergies in much the same way that people can. Not only can the Shiba Inu develop allergies to certain food ingredients, but he can also develop inhalant or contact allergies. The general signs of allergies include the following:

- Itchy red skin
- Itchy or runny eyes
- Licking the base of the tail
- Sneezing or coughing
- Ear infections
- Diarrhea
- Snoring from throat inflammation

- Chewing the paws

Some of the things that the Shiba Inu can be allergic to include grass, weeds, pollen, mold spores, dust, dander, feathers, cigarette smoke, prescription drugs, perfumes, and cleaning products. They can also be allergic to certain flea and tick products, so be very careful about which one you choose. You should also never use products on your dog that are not designed specifically for dogs – this includes shampoo.

One of the most common complaints discussed at the veterinarian's office when they see dogs obsessively scratching, biting, licking, and chewing at their skin or paws is possible allergies, and there can be many triggers. When you educate yourself, you can help ensure your Shiba Inu never has to suffer from allergies and can lead a healthier and happier life.

Spaying and Neutering

There are a lot of factors to consider when deciding if you should spay or neuter your puppy. Many owners refuse to spay or neuter their puppy because they find it morally wrong and unnatural. However, most owners do decide to have their pet neutered. Shelter euthanasia is the number one killer of dogs and companion animals throughout America. In Atlanta, alone over 15 million dollars is spent annually on euthanizing unwanted dogs! The only way to avoid this is to have your pet spayed or neutered. Dogs face some discomfort if they are in heat or are unable to mate. Spaying and neutering create no long-term health problems for your pet. At the end of the day, it is an important decision for you and your family to make. I advise talking it over with your vet and family/friends who have already been through the process.

Pet Health Insurance

Purchasing health insurance for your dog means that they will usually live a longer, healthier, and happier life because they will receive better care throughout their lifetime.

Be aware that it's a better idea to begin insurance when your dog is a young puppy because waiting until they are older will mean that your monthly premiums are considerably higher.

Chapter Seven: Vet Care for Your Shiba Inu

Chapter Eight: Showing Your Shiba Inu

Showing your Shiba Inu can be a wonderful experience for both you and your pet. In training your dog, you will develop a closer relationship with him, and your dog may enjoy the experience as well.

For purebreds like the Shiba Inu, there are many opportunities for show. One of the most prestigious dog shows in the United States is the Westminster Kennel Club Dog Show which is held in Madison Square Garden in New York City each year. This two-day show is an all-breed benched competition for conformation. In the U.K., one of the top dog shows for purebreds is Crufts. This show is open to all kinds of dogs including.

Chapter Eight: Showing Your Shiba Inu

Showing Shiba Inu Dogs

As long as your Shiba Inu is at least six months old, and AKC or UK KC registered, has no disqualifying faults, it can be shown. Spaying is a grey area, as it has generally been considered that neutered dogs cannot be shown. This is not entirely true as the KC for example, has allowed such cases. You should check this with your local Kennel Club. Winning at your fist show is very difficult. There is much to learn about the show world, and you'll need to be very prepared before you start showing your Shiba Inu.

Shiba Inus are one of the easiest breeds to show. You will need to attend many dog shows before both you and your Shiba Inu give a polished performance. There are also professional dog handlers that could show your Shiba Inu for you.

To get more information on showing, you'll need to contact your local kennel club and see if they have any handling classes or when the next show is. These are informal and casual events where all dog owners learn. These include puppies, handlers, and even judges. Losses and wins at these matches should be taken lightly. Even at a serious show, dog handlers and owners should try not to get too serious. The results are the judge's decision.

When competing at a real AKC show, every time the judge chooses your Shiba Inu as the best male or female Shiba Inu, it does not mean he or she is a Champion. Your dog wins up to 5 points. This depends on how many other dogs it defeats.

Chapter Eight: Showing Your Shiba Inu

How To Become an AKC Champion

Your Shiba Inu must win 15 points including 2 majors. This means defeating enough dogs to win 3 to 5 points at a time. As a competitor, you're allowed to enter any class that your Shiba Inu is eligible for: Puppy, Novice. American Bred, Bred by Exhibitor, or Open. The Best of Breed class is for dogs that are already Champions.

This is a brief example and rules can change from time to time. Please check your countries Kennel Club for the latest rule changes and updates.

What to Know Before You Show

If you plan to show your Shiba Inu dog, there are a few things you need to know before you register. The exact rules and requirements will vary from one show to another, so pay attention to specific requirements. Before you attempt to show your Shiba Inu, make sure your dog meets the following requirements:

- Your dog needs to be fully house-trained, and able to hold his bladder for several hours.
- Your Shiba Inu needs to be properly socialized, and able to get along well with both humans and other dogs.
- Your dog should have basic obedience training, and he should respond consistently to your commands and look to you for leadership.

Chapter Eight: Showing Your Shiba Inu

- Your Shiba Inu should be even-tempered, not aggressive or hyperactive in public settings.
- Your dog needs to meet the specific eligibility requirements of whatever show you are participating in. There may be certain requirements for age, for example.
- Your Shiba Inu needs to be completely up to date on his vaccinations so there is no risk of him contracting or spreading disease among other dogs at the show.

In addition to considering these requirements, you also need to make sure that you yourself are prepared for the show.

The list below will help you to know what to bring with you on the day of the show:

- Your dog's registration information
- A dog crate and exercise pen
- Food and water bowls for your dog
- Your dog's food and treats
- Grooming supplies and grooming table
- Trash bags for cleanup
- Any medications your dog needs
- A change of clothes for yourself
- Food and water for yourself
- Paper towels or rags for cleanup

Chapter Eight: Showing Your Shiba Inu

- Toys to keep your dog occupied

Preparing Your Dog for Show

Your preparations for the dog show will vary according to the type of show in which you have entered. If you enter an obedience show for example, perfecting your dog's appearance may be less important than it would for a conformation show. Before you even enter your dog into a show you should consider attending a few dog shows yourself to get a feel for it. Walk around the tent where the dogs are being prepared for show and pay close attention during the judging to learn what the judges are looking for in any given show. The more you learn before you show your own dog, the better off you will be. One of the most important things you need to do in preparation for a conformation show is to have your Shiba Inu properly groomed so that his coat is in good condition.

Follow the steps below to groom your Shiba Inu in preparation for show:

- The night before the show, give your Shiba Inu a thorough brushing then trim his nails and clean his ears as well.
- Give your dog a bath and dry his coat thoroughly before brushing him again.
- Once your dog is clean, you need to keep him that way. Have him sleep in a crate that night and keep him on the leash during his morning walk.

Chapter Eight: Showing Your Shiba Inu

- The day of the show, brush your Shiba Inu's coat again.
- When you arrive at the show, keep your dog in his crate or in a fenced exercise pen so he doesn't get dirty.

When it comes time for judging, just remember that the main reason you are doing this is to have fun with your dog. Do not get too upset if your Shiba Inu does not win. Just take notes of ways you can improve for the next show and enjoy the experience you and your dog had together that day.

Chapter Nine: Breeding Your Shiba Inu

Breeding your Shiba Inu is an important decision that every dog owner should make before they purchase a puppy. While we often think of breeding after the purchase, by choosing to breed beforehand, you can ensure that you are starting with the very best dog you can find.

Remember to read the chapter on choosing a puppy in this book. One thing that will help you is to find a mentor in the breed before you decide to breed your dog. Breeding an Shiba Inu is a constant learning experience and it will help you to know someone in the breed who has years of experience.

This chapter will provide you with tips on choosing the right dogs for your breeding program, how and when to

Chapter Nine: Breeding Your Shiba Inu

breed, the simple facts about whelping a puppy, and the schedule for raising puppies.

Choosing Dogs To Breed

The very first thing that you should do before deciding to breed your Shiba Inus is to select the right dogs. While every dog can be bred, not every dog should be bred. It is important to really understand the breed standard of the Shiba Inu before you breed.

If you are interested in breeding professionally, you will probably want to find a "breeding pair" – a male and female Shiba Inu. However, most people who breed as a hobby or breed to show their dogs look for the best male or female dog they can find. They usually seek the best female dog if they want to breed a litter. That's because they can use stud dogs owned by other breeders without tying themselves to the same male forever.

If you have a good female dog, you will likely want to choose a different mate for her each time. That way you can see what kind of puppies she produces with different dogs or different bloodlines. If you are serious about being a dog breeder, you need to think in terms of generations. Having two or three litters from your girl from different bloodlines could give you the best start for the future, assuming you will be keeping a puppy from a litter for yourself.

In general, when you are choosing a dog for breeding, you want to look at the following:

Chapter Nine: Breeding Your Shiba Inu

Health

Dogs should be healthy and in good condition. They should be in proportionate weight for their build and also pass a health test from your vet. They should be free of disease so there is no risk of that disease being passed along to the young.

If the vet voices any concerns over the health of the dogs, wait to breed them until they are in better health or choose different dogs.

Clearances

Health clearances are very important to ensure the health of your puppies and the lifelong health of any dog you produce. Shiba Inus have several genetic diseases which are discussed in the chapter on health. You should familiarize yourself with these health issues and the tests for them.

In addition to these clearances, you should have the dogs tested for brucellosis, which is a canine STD. Any dog that is being bred should be clear. Brucellosis can cause sterility in both males and females and can cause the dam to abort the puppies.

Registration

Before buying any dog for breeding, you should make sure the dog is registered with the kennel club you desire, or eligible to be registered.

Temperament

Temperament is as important as health when it comes to breeding. Studies have proven that temperament is an hereditary trait so it is important to breed dogs with a sound temperament. If you have a dog with aggression or skittishness, it is recommended that you do not breed the dog.

Bloodlines

Another factor that you want to take into account is the blood line. Is it a strong pedigree? When considering pedigrees for breeding it is particularly important to have a mentor or someone you trust give you some advice. Linebreeding, outcrossing, and other breeding theories, as well as just reading pedigrees takes some practice to understand them.

Age

Something that is very important with breeding is the age of the dogs. Females should be no younger than 18 months of age for breeding and males should not be younger than 15 months of age. Ideally, you won't breed a male or female before they have had at least preliminary hip x-rays so you can be reasonably certain they do not have hip dysplasia. Some health tests cannot be done until the dog is older.

On the other end of the age spectrum, you should not breed a bitch after she is 7 years of age. Males can be bred for many years after that; however, the quality and quantity of sperm can be affected by age.

Chapter Nine: Breeding Your Shiba Inu

Physical Traits

Finally, you will want to choose dogs according to their physical traits. While the dogs you select should be good examples of the breed, you should look at what each dog can bring to their future puppies.

For instance, if both dogs have excellent paws according to the breed standard, the odds are very high that the puppies will inherit those paws. A good coat on a female may be passed on to the puppies, even if the male has a coat that is not as good. A good body shape on the male may be passed on to the puppies and so on. Just remember that sometimes bad traits are passed on instead of the good ones.

Choosing complementary traits will only improve your puppies and your lines. While many people promote showing, it is not a prerequisite for breeding. However, showing your dogs does have benefits for breeding dogs. It puts you in touch with a community of reputable breeders. It allows you to see many Shiba Inus and compare traits. It keeps you informed about dog matters. So, it has advantages for anyone interested in breeding dogs.

Before you do make that final decision about which dogs to breed, it is important to remember that breeding is a responsibility. There is often very little money to be earned when doing it properly and it is a full-time commitment.

While the dam will help with the care, there is a lot to be done during those 8 (or more) weeks that you will be raising puppies at home. In addition, breeders should be

Chapter Nine: Breeding Your Shiba Inu

prepared to re-home any of their puppies if they are returned for some reason.

Breeding is not for the faint of heart by any means but one thing is certain: cuddling a newborn Shiba Inu in your hands is worth all the work, money and commitment.

Before breeding your female dog, we recommend that you make sure she is up-to-date on her vaccinations. The mother dog will be able to pass along temporary immunity to common dog diseases to her puppies when they are born so you want to make sure her own immunity is at its maximum. In the UK and Europe we also recommend that bitches receive the canine herpes virus vaccination before breeding. Canine herpes virus is extremely widespread, affecting up to 90 percent of all dogs. It is harmless to most adult dogs but, under stress, it can kill newborn puppies. The vaccine is very helpful in protecting the newborns. Unfortunately, this vaccine is not available at this time in the United States.

Breeding your Shiba Inu

Now that you have chosen the dogs you wish to breed, it is time to breed your dog. While it may seem like a simple thing, breeding an Shiba Inu can be challenging. Dogs usually know how to mate (usually), but there is a lot you need to know to have a successful litter.

Chapter Nine: Breeding Your Shiba Inu

The Heat

When a female dog reaches sexual maturity, she will begin what is known as a heat. A heat or heat cycle is when the female will begin bleeding and will be ready to accept the male within a few days. For Shiba Inus, the first heat is usually between six months and a year; however, a dog should never be bred on her first heat or before the age of around 18 months.

With heat cycles, some females will take longer to have their first heat and it is not uncommon for an Shiba Inu to be closer to a year of age or even up to 2 years when she has her first heat. Most domestic dogs today come in season once or twice a year – anywhere from every six to 14 months. Some bitches have a regular cycle while others are more erratic. One thing is certain: when you are waiting for your girl to come in season so you can breed her, she will seem to take longer. She will most likely come in season at the worst possible time. For some reason, that's just how the timing always seems to work out. You will be trying to make arrangements to breed her while your family shakes their heads at your dog obsession.

With heat cycles, signs of the heat begin before the discharge. Often the vulva begins to swell and the female will begin licking her back end and vulva more. In addition, she may be urinating more frequently and if you have any male dogs in the home, you may notice them paying more attention to her than usual.

The female will begin to have a bloody discharge and this can vary in heaviness between females and even heats. Some females have very little discharge and other females have a lot. Females are not ready to breed at this time. The discharge will gradually become paler until it is a straw color. This usually takes around 2 to 11 days. This is when the female is ready to breed. Young male dogs may not be able to tell the difference but experienced stud dogs often won't bother spending much time with a female until she is actually ready to breed.

The entire heat cycle lasts about 3 weeks but it is important to not let the female near a male until about 4 weeks after the start of her heat if you do not want her to breed. If you are planning on breeding her, breeding will take place about 9 to 11 days after her heat starts.

Natural or Artificial?

When you are breeding, you can choose between allowing the dogs to breed naturally or to carry out an AI (Artificial Insemination) breeding. Many breeders learn how to do AIs themselves. However, in the event of frozen sperm, you would need to have the AI done by a veterinarian, specifically a reproductive veterinarian. Frozen sperm is often shipped to a breeder by another breeder from a long distance, at considerable expense. You do not want to take any chances that the insemination might fail.

Natural breeding is when you allow the male dog to mount the female and achieve a tie. This is often the more preferred way to breed.

With AI, the sperm is delivered to the vagina through a sterilized tube. There are several reasons why you would use AI and these are:

a) Stud dog is too far away.
b) A dominant female who will not allow a male to mount.
c) Inexperienced stud dog.
d) A persistent hymen in a bitch.
e) Size incompatibility

AI is less likely to spread an STD but it usually accounts for smaller litter sizes. Also, it is important to properly judge when ovulation occurs, which can be difficult and is usually done with progesterone testing by your vet.

Many breeders use AI with fresh semen, even when the stud dog is on the premises. This is done to avoid any injury to the stud dog and to avoid any chance of passing disease.

When to Breed

You have the stud dog, a bitch in heat and you have made the decision to go with a natural tie. Terrific, you are ready to start breeding soon ... but maybe not right away.

Breeding times differs from female to female, although the general rule of thumb is between days 9 and 11. If you have the male in the home, you can begin breeding as soon as the female starts accepting him.

Chapter Nine: Breeding Your Shiba Inu

The rule of thumb, however, is to breed every other day. This gives the sperm time to recover in numbers and you will have better sperm numbers. (Male dogs have sperm in the millions.)

If you do not have a male, you can do progesterone testing to try to narrow down when your female is most fertile. Progesterone testing is done with a blood test, however, you can also do a vaginal smear, although this is not as accurate.

When using progesterone testing, follow the guidelines of your veterinarian.

Although testing the dog is an excellent way to identify if your female dog is ready to be bred, you can also see this with her behavior. A female that is ready to be bred will exhibit the following:

a) Vaginal discharge will turn to a light pink or straw color.
b) The female will back up into the male.
c) She will hold her tail to the side. This is known as flagging.
d) She will be playful with the male.
e) She will stand still when the male is sniffing her.
f) She won't attack the male when he tries to mount her.

When you see these signs, your female is ready to be bred. Even with these signs, however, progesterone testing can be more accurate for determining the exact right time for mating. There is a spike in the LH (luteinizing hormone) 48 hours prior to ovulation. This spike will trigger the

Chapter Nine: Breeding Your Shiba Inu

progesterone levels to begin rising, signaling the best times for breeding. After the LH surge and the rise in progesterone, do a natural breeding three days later, for example. The sperm in fresh semen can survive 5 to 7 days in the female dog's uterus.

Artificial insemination using fresh chilled semen can be used four days after the rise in progesterone. Sperm in chilled semen survive 48 to 72 hours after insemination.

Artificial insemination using frozen semen can be used five days after the progesterone surge. Sperm in frozen semen only survives 24 hours once it is deposited in the uterus by surgical means after insemination.

The Act of Breeding

When your female is ready to be bred, it is time to let the dogs do their job. During this time, you should allow the stud dog and the bitch to be together. Never leave them unattended as injuries can occur if the female attacks the male or she becomes scared.

The stud dog will spend some time sniffing the rear of the female and he may begin to lick the vulva. The female will stand still and will move her tail out of the way. She will also back into the male.

Note, if you have a maiden bitch or an inexperienced stud dog, you can have success without intervening, but things often go much better if you are on hand to assist.

Chapter Nine: Breeding Your Shiba Inu

Inexperienced stud dogs can sometimes be so excited that they will mount the wrong end of the girl, for example. Maiden girls are not always sure what that pesky boy has in mind. The dogs usually figure things out but if you have invested a lot of money in a stud fee or driven a long way with your girl, sometimes it helps if you or the stud dog owner lends a guiding hand. You can hold the bitch in position or guide the boy in the right direction, for example.

If you have an experienced bitch and/or stud dog, they usually know what they are doing and things go smoothly and quickly when the time is right.

As the male builds excitement, he will mount the female, wrapping his front legs around the hips of the female.

He will begin to thrust against the female and his penis will enter the vulva.

During this action, the glans penis will come out of the sheath, which is a bright red organ. The penis will extend into the vulva until the dog locks with the female. Once the lock happens, the male and female cannot be separated. Do not try to separate them as you can hurt both the male and the female.

Once he is locked, the male will often lift his leg over the rear of the female and then turn so they are standing with their back ends together. The penis will bend but will still be inserted in the vulva.

Dogs will remain usually remain locked for 10 to 30 minutes until the penis loses some of its swelling so it is released from the lock.

Chapter Nine: Breeding Your Shiba Inu

One myth that abounds is that a female cannot get pregnant if there is no tie. This is not true. When the dog is thrusting, sperm is released. The fluid that is released when they are locked is very low in sperm and is used to push the sperm through the cervix. Only allow your dogs to mate once per day and then wait a day before you breed again.

Is She Pregnant?

The gestational period for dogs is between the 63 to 65 days after the time of first breeding, however, you can have some additional or fewer days depending on the individual dog and breeding. If you have used progesterone testing, whelping is nearly always exactly 63 days after ovulation. Even if you have bred your dogs late in the heat, you can count on 63 days from ovulation rather than from the date of the breeding.

One of the biggest worries that breeders go through is whether a dog is pregnant. This is very difficult to determine because a female dog goes through the same hormone changes whether she is pregnant or not. In fact, even a female who has not been bred can present the symptoms of pregnancy.

During the first month, you will notice very few signs. The female may have morning sickness where her appetite decreases, however, some females are not affected at all.

After the first 30 days, the dog will begin to show some symptoms. Symptoms of pregnancy are:

Chapter Nine: Breeding Your Shiba Inu

a) Nipple Growth
b) Pinking of the Nipples
c) Decreased Appetite early on
d) Increased Appetite around week 6
e) Clinginess and other behavior changes
f) Pear shape of the abdomen
g) Weight gain

At 30 to 35 days, you can have an ultrasound done to confirm pregnancy. Numbers are not usually given during ultrasounds as it is very difficult to count the puppies. Experienced vets and breeders can often palpate a bitch's abdomen and feel puppies. At 30 days puppies are about the size of walnuts. After this time they can't be felt again for several weeks. After 45-50 days gestation, an x-ray can be done and the puppies can be counted at that time. It is important to note that sometimes counts are wrong since puppies will hide in the x-ray. It is a good idea to have an x-ray done so you will know how many puppies to expect. This helps you know when your girl is finished whelping.

To answer a common question: No, you cannot use a human pregnancy test to determine if your bitch is pregnant. The hormone levels are not the same for dogs as they are for humans. There is a pregnancy test for dogs but it is not accurate until about 30 days – or the same time that you can do an ultrasound or palpate the puppies.

During pregnancy you can continue to feed your female her normal dog food for the first six weeks. After this time, you can begin to increase her food. You can add some pre-natal vitamins to her diet but do not add any additional calcium or other supplements at this time. You can switch her to an all-life stage dog food, or a puppy food at this time since she will be using the extra calories as the puppies develop. Once the puppies are born, you can feed your female dog as much as she wants to eat, especially if she has several puppies. She will need the extra calories to produce milk.

Whelping your Pups

So your female Shiba Inu is pregnant and the time is drawing closer to when you will be whelping her puppies. This is an exciting time but it is also a busy time for you. It is very important to have all your supplies ready and to begin preparing for the puppies a few weeks before their arrival.

Whelping Supplies

The first thing that is important to have on hand are the whelping supplies. These are essential for helping your puppies and mother. In the best-case scenario, you will need to interact very little with the labor. In the worst case, you could be looking at having to rush your pregnant dog to the vet clinic for an emergency c-section.

In addition, even an easy whelping can result in puppies in distress so it is important to have the tools on hand to help the puppies. Things you will need in your whelping supplies are:

Chapter Nine: Breeding Your Shiba Inu

- **Whelping Box:** This should be a square or rectangular box that the mother can deliver and raise her puppies in. You can make the box yourself or you can purchase pre-made whelping boxes. The box does need to be sturdy and good quality since you will be cleaning it frequently. This will be the puppies' home for the next few weeks.
- **Blankets:** Have a lot of blankets on hand for your whelping box. Labor is messy and that means you have to exchange the bedding in the whelping box several times during labor.
- **Newspaper:** In addition to blankets, have a large amount of newspaper to put down during the whelping process. Again, you are going to be going through a lot of it. You can also get end rolls from your local newspaper. These are clean paper rolls without the ink. They aren't nearly as messy as newspaper.
- **Basket:** A laundry basket or Tupperware container to put the puppies in when the female is birthing another puppy.
- **Hot Water Bottles:** Water bottles are needed for the basket so puppies can stay warm when they are not with their mother. Puppies will cuddle up to the water bottles if they are cold and will move away if they are too warm. You can also use a heating pad, but wrap it with a towel so the puppies don't get burned on it.
- **Scale:** Have a kitchen scale so you can properly weigh each puppy as it is born. This will be a tool you use throughout the time the litter is with you since you will want to weigh the puppies on a regular basis.

- **Notebook and Pens:** Create a notebook that charts the progress of each individual puppy. Start with the puppies' sex, identifier, date of birth, presentation at birth, time born, coloration and weight. This will help you keep track of each puppy.
- **Identifier:** This can be yarn, puppy collars, or nail polish for their nails. Basically, it is anything that you can use to identify each puppy. Use the yarn like a collar on each puppy so you can identify each individual puppy right from birth. Use the same collar color for that puppy throughout the 8 weeks that you have the puppies.

In addition to those items, have the following items available in a kit. Be sure to sterilize all of the instruments such as the scissors and hemostats:

a) Sharp Scissors
b) Hemostats
c) Surgical Gloves
d) Iodine Swabs
e) Alcohol Swabs
f) Lubricating Jelly such as K-Y
g) Digital Thermometer
h) Vaseline
i) Nursing Bottles for Puppies
j) Liquid Puppy Vitamins
k) Puppy Formula
l) Energizing Glucose Drops
m) Bulb Syringe

Place all of the items into an easy to access container and have it close to your whelping box.

Before Labor

As you know, the gestation period for dogs is about 63 days, give or take a few days. However, it is important to monitor your dog during the days leading up to the delivery. Around day 56 to 58, the female should start searching for a nesting site. Encourage her to nest in the whelping box by sitting next to it and calmly petting her. Do not discourage her scratching at the bedding as this is normal.

In addition to this, you should start taking her temperature about a week before her due date. The average temperature of your female will be between 99 to 101°F (37.22 to 38.33°C). Mark down her temperature each day and, closer to the due date, start checking her temperature several times per day.

The reason why we are watching the temperature is because we are waiting for a temperature spike and then drop. About 48 hours before labor, her temperature will have a spike up to about 101.5°F (38.6°C) or higher. Within 24 hours after that, the temperature will drop. Once it gets to below 98°F (36.7°C), you will have between 12 to 24 hours before the litter is expected.

First Stage Labor

When she has her final temp drop, you will start to notice a number of signs that your female is going into labor.

Chapter Nine: Breeding Your Shiba Inu

For about 2 to 12 hours, your female will become restless. She may start to nest even more than she did before, or she may become very stressed wanting to wander around the house.

You may see some shivering and she will probably change positions frequently. Her eyes will dilate and she will watch you and want to be with you. Try to stay near the whelping box so she can settle in.

She may lose her appetite during this time and it is not uncommon for your Shiba Inu female to vomit. Also, she may try to go to the bathroom and not be able to. This is caused by the pressure building up in her stomach.

If you take your Shiba Inu outside to go to the bathroom, keep her on a leash and check the spot where she squatted. It is not uncommon for puppies to be born outside.

Finally, you may see some mucus being discharged from the vulva.

Second Stage of Labor

During the second stage of labor, your female should start digging at her bedding even more. You will also notice your Shiba Inu looking at her back end more frequently and she may start licking her vulva.

Shivering is more noticeable and she will have periods where she is panting heavily. You may be able to see mild contractions going across her belly or you may feel a tightening of her stomach.

Again, your Shiba Inu may vomit and she may ask to go outside more frequently. Remember to stay with her when she goes to the bathroom to make sure a pup is not born outside.

At this time, if the discharge turns to a dark green color, seek medical help. Dark green discharge is normal but only after a puppy is born. If it is before, it can indicate a life-threatening problem for both your bitch and your litter.

Third Stage of Labor

This is the stage of labor when the puppies begin to be whelped. During this time, the contractions will become stronger and you will be able to see them. They will also occur closer together.

Your Shiba Inu female may vomit during this time and you will notice that she will begin pushing and grunting. Some females will squat when they have their puppies, others will lay on their side so let the female decide how she is going to birth the puppy.

As she is pushing, you will see a membrane sac filled with water and the puppy come out of the vulva. Puppies are born in their own sac and it may burst while being delivered or as the female breaks it.

In addition, puppies are born both front feet first and breech, with their tail or back feet presented first. The puppy is followed by the afterbirth. Females often eat the afterbirth as it contains hormones to stimulate milk production. Count each afterbirth after the puppies are born to make sure each

Chapter Nine: Breeding Your Shiba Inu

one is expelled. A retained afterbirth can cause a serious infection and lead to complications for your female.

Puppies are usually born in quick succession of two or three puppies, then you will have a wait of about an hour or so before additional puppies are born.

The process of birthing can last up to 24 hours, depending on the size of the litter.

If you find that the female is pushing for longer than 30 minutes without seeing a puppy, contact your veterinarian and follow his advice. It could mean a puppy is caught.

Also, if there is a long period of time between puppies, contact your veterinarian, especially if you are expecting more puppies.

When the puppies are born, allow them to nurse from their mother between births. Every time she is ready to push, remove the puppies to your basket. This keeps her from being distracted by the puppies and she is less likely to sit on the puppy or hurt it. Try to let her do the work herself. If you get too involved, you could cause her to stop laboring. Only get involved if she looks like she needs help.

In between puppies, weigh the puppy that was recently born, jot down all the notes on the puppy and place an identifier collar on the puppy.

Watching a litter being born is a very exciting thing but make sure you are prepared for any problems. Also, keep the whelping room quiet and calm.

Chapter Nine: Breeding Your Shiba Inu

It is also important to note that in the weeks after giving birth, the gland that is responsible for regulating the parathyroid hormone, which in turn regulates the amount of calcium which is stored within the mother, can become depleted.

When the bitch's milk starts to come in, and the demand for calcium suddenly is increased, the parathyroid gland is unable to respond quickly enough for her needs to be fully met. This can lead to her body contracting convulsively, which effectively will limit her movement. This condition is known as eclampsia.

Once diagnosed with eclampsia, the new mother will be prescribed calcium supplementation. Alternatively, foods such as Cottage Cheese, Goats Milk, or Mature Cheddar will also help in supporting her to heal through this phase.

If your female becomes fatigued during delivery or seems to be stalled, you can provide her with some vanilla ice cream for energy and calcium support.

After whelping, be sure she eats and has plenty of fresh water. You can offer her some chicken or broth if her appetite is off. She should soon be hungry again since she will be nursing a litter of puppies.

Raising Puppies

Raising pups is a fun activity and, for the first few weeks, the mother does the majority of the work. She will clean the puppies and feed them. However, it does not mean that you have nothing to do - you will be very busy with your own

Chapter Nine: Breeding Your Shiba Inu

chores. Below is a chart of what you need to do with the puppies while they are growing.

Week 1

The puppies sleep the majority of the time. When they are awake, they will crawl towards warmth and milk. The puppies have their eyes and ears closed and are helpless at this age.

a) Chart weight twice a day.

b) Trim nails at the end of the week.

c) Handle the puppies daily to check their health and start neurological stimulation.

d) Clean the bedding daily.

e) Monitor the mother and her health.

f) Keep the whelping box temperature about 85°F (29.4°C).

Week 2

Puppies are beginning to move around more and they are awake for longer periods.

a) Trim nails at the end of the week.

b) Hold the puppies in different positions to accustom them to being handled.

c) Monitor the mother and her health.

Chapter Nine: Breeding Your Shiba Inu

d) Clean bedding daily.

e) Weigh puppies once a day.

Eyes and ears

Eyes will begin to open at 8 - 10 days and ears will open near the end of week 2 or the start of week 3.

Week 3

Eyes and ears will be open by the end of this week and the pups will be more active. They will start trying to walk and go to the bathroom without stimulation from mother. They will begin to play and their little teeth will be starting to show.

a) Continue to handle the puppies.

b) Trim nails at end of the week.

c) Begin getting the pups familiar with items such as grooming brushes and combs.

d) Weigh puppies every other day.

e) Monitor the mother and her health.

f) Begin weaning process.

g) Start with milk replacer once a day for two days.

h) Then add a mushy food once per day.

i) Clean bedding daily.

Week 4

Chapter Nine: Breeding Your Shiba Inu

During this week, the puppies will be more playful and begin growling. They will also be eating mushy food and nurse occasionally.

Their mother will be resting more and feeding less, but should still be with them a lot. As soon as they start eating foods other than their mother's milk, cleaning up dog mess will be your job.

a) Continue to handle the puppies.

b) Trim nails at end of the week.

c) Begin familiarizing the puppies to other things such as noises and other animals in your home.

d) Weigh puppies every other day.

e) Monitor the mother and her health.

f) Shift the food to be the consistency of porridge and add one extra meal a day.

g) Clean bedding daily.

Week 5

Puppies are more alert and they will be active. You will start to see temperament emerging, and may even see sexual play. Puppies grow quickly during this time.

a) Weigh puppies two to three times each week.

b) Reduce the mother's diet to stop her milk production.

c) Start reducing the amount of liquid in the puppies' food.

Chapter Nine: Breeding Your Shiba Inu

d) Continue to handle the puppies.

e) Trim nails at end of the week.

f) Continue getting the puppies accustomed to a range of stimuli.

g) Clean bedding daily.

Week 6

Puppies are developing quickly and showing signs of their own personalities. Mother will spend less time with the puppies at this stage.

a) Give each puppy time alone.

b) Weigh the puppies weekly.

c) Continue reducing the amount of liquid in the puppies' food.

d) Continue to handle the puppies.

e) Trim nails at end of the week.

f) Continue widening the puppies' range of stimuli.

g) Clean bedding daily.

Week 7

Puppies will be able to hear and see fully at this stage. They will be very inquisitive and can get into some problems if you just take your eyes off them for a second.

a) Give each puppy time alone.

Chapter Nine: Breeding Your Shiba Inu

b) Weigh the puppies weekly.
c) Puppies should be fully weaned and on puppy food.
d) Continue to handle the puppies.
e) Trim nails at end of the week.
f) Continue socializing the puppies to a range of stimuli.
g) Clean bedding daily.

Week 8

Puppies are at the age where they can start going to their new homes. This is the week when a fear period can occur so make sure you do not stress them too much.

a) Give each puppy some time alone.
b) Weigh the puppies weekly.
c) Trim nails at end of the week.
d) Continue socializing the puppies to a range of stimuli.
e) Clean bedding daily.
f) Start training puppies that have not already left for their new home.

Raising a litter of puppies is a lot of work so before you breed your Shiba Inu, it is important to do a lot of research and be ready for the commitment. Any breeder will also tell you that it is advisable to have homes lined up for the puppies before you breed, or at least to know how you will place your puppies.

Chapter Nine: Breeding Your Shiba Inu

Shiba Inu puppies may be highly desirable but it is still necessary to let people know you are breeding a litter. You will want to make sure your puppies are going to good homes after you have put so much work into breeding the litter and raising them. Most breeders have a waiting list and take deposits on their puppies when they are born.

Puppy Development

As you raise new puppies, they will go through certain developmental stages. There are seven stages during which time the Shiba Inu puppies will develop mentally and physically.

It is important to note that the following facts apply to all newborn Shiba Inu puppies:

a) All puppies are born blind, deaf, and without teeth
b) All puppies are born unable to produce body heat
c) New puppies will grunt, cry, or whine whenever they are unhappy, uncomfortable, cold, or hungry
d) Rapid development mentally and physically will take place during the first eight weeks
e)

Stage 1

This is the period from birth to three weeks of age.

During these three weeks, these Shiba Inu puppies will spend most of their time sleeping. This enables them to grow.

Chapter Nine: Breeding Your Shiba Inu

Generally, ninety percent of the time will be spent sleeping with the remaining ten percent spent eating. At this point the puppies can only crawl. They will begin to crawl by week two. Their eyes will open between nine and twelve days. At this point, they will only be able to see shadows. They ears will open between twelve and seventeen days.

Stage 2

This is the period between three and seven weeks of age.

At the three-week mark, their teeth will begin to appear. They will also start their first socialization with other puppies from the litter. They will start to take their first steps, and develop of sense of smell. Soon, they will begin to bark. At this point, their mother will spend more time with them than she has to date.

Between four and seven weeks of age, most mothers will begin to wean their pups. Their mother will begin to teach them correct behavior and by four weeks, the mother will start to leave the puppies for longer periods. They should begin to walk quite well at this point. Soon, you will see a pack order being established among the litter.

The puppies will learn to bite at this point, but the litter mates and mother will teach the puppy when it is acceptable to bite down hard and when it is not. This is why puppies must remain with the breeder until at least seven weeks old. Breeders who are licensed by the USDA must keep puppies until they are 8 weeks of age. Show and hobby breeders in the

Chapter Nine: Breeding Your Shiba Inu

United States may or may not need to be licensed by the United States Department of Agriculture, depending on many different factors.

At seven weeks the puppy will begin exploration and receive its first immunization.

During these weeks the breeder should be handling puppies often and socializing them at home.

Stage 3

This is the period between seven and twelve weeks of age.

Fear begins to develop at this stage but this will wane by week twelve. The puppy will begin to learn human voices at this point, and start house training. You will notice that Shiba Inu puppies will begin to explore for longer periods of time at this point and will start to develop finer motor skills. The puppy will receive its second round of immunizations once it hits nine weeks of age.

If you plan on taking your Shiba Inu puppy to obedience classes, it will need its kennel cough immunization at this point as well.

Stage 4

This is the period between twelve and sixteen weeks of age.

Chapter Nine: Breeding Your Shiba Inu

This stage is where the Shiba Inu puppy receives its third round of immunizations. This is also where permanent teeth begin to break through. As a result, the puppy will start to chew on many types of toys with a variety of textures. Their gums may be quite sore during this stage. The Shiba Inu puppy should receive its immunization for rabies in the U.S. during this time.

Stage 5

This is the period from four to eight months of age.

This period of development is the same as the teenage years for adults. It is a time period where consistency in training is imperative, as the Shiba Inu puppy will often try and ignore or challenge you. At this stage, they will chew on anything they can get their mouths on, but their permanent teeth come in around six months of age. At this stage, they require many chewable toys.

Their confidence will increase at this point, and as a result, they will want to play independently more often. They may go through a second fear period between six months and fourteen months. This varies by dog.

Stage 6

This is the period from eight months to one year of age.

This is the during which puppies will mature sexually and may challenge your authority even more than before.

Chapter Nine: Breeding Your Shiba Inu

During this period the Shiba Inu puppy will be safe to jump, as their joints will reach full development. They will look like an adult dog but still act like a puppy. Their height will develop fully during this stage, but their chest, back, and legs may still grow.

Stage 7

This is the period from one year to eighteen months of age.

This is the point at which your Shiba Inu is considered an adult. They will reach their full growth by the first birthday and may start to forget all that you taught them between twelve and eighteen months, but have no fear, as they will eventually remember those early lessons.

Conclusion

To get the best out of raising and training your Shiba Inu, you'll first have to get to know his unique character and personality. Getting to know your Shiba Inu on a truly personal level is of utmost importance if you're going to realize any measure of success in raising and training him — and develop a lasting and loving bond.

A happy and healthy Shiba Inu is one that offers the best companionship. A well-trained Shiba Inu makes for a great addition to the family. In order to keep your Shiba Inu happy and healthy, you have to pay attention to some Shiba Inu-specific care-giving requirements, such as their genetic predisposition to certain health issues, their special grooming needs and how much exercise they need in relation to their inherently high energy levels, among a lot of other things.

A happy and healthy Shiba Inu is also one that can be trained with relatively greater ease. Successfully training your Shiba Inu ultimately comes down to relating your commands to an action you want him to complete or an object you want him to interact with, making use of the four characteristics you have identified in your specific Shiba Inu: his likes, dislikes, temperament, and energy levels. With this approach in mind, you can train your Shiba Inu to achieve pretty much anything you want him to and thereby get the very best out of your Shiba Inu as a family member and companion.

Conclusion

Glossary of Terms

Adoption – A process in which a rescued pet is placed into a permanent home.

Acute Disease – refers to a disease or illness that manifests quickly

Agility – This is a sport in which the dog handler guides and instructs the dog through a course of obstacles while being timed. Accuracy through this obstacle course is paramount. The dogs must complete the obstacle course without a leash or toys (or food) as incentives. The handler can only use voice, movement and various body signals in order to direct the dog.

AKC – American Kennel Club, the largest purebred dog registry in the United States

Almond Eye – Referring to an elongated eye shape rather than a rounded shape

Apple Head – A round-shaped skull

Balance – A show term referring to all of the parts of the dog, both moving and standing, which produce a harmonious image

Beard – Long, thick hair on the dog's underjaw

Best in Show – An award given to the only undefeated dog left standing at the end of judging

Bitch – A female dog

Glossary of Terms

Bite – The position of the upper and lower teeth when the dog's jaws are closed; positions include level, undershot, scissors, or overshot

Blaze – A white stripe running down the center of the face between the eyes

Board – To house, feed, and care for a dog for a fee

Breed – A domestic race of dogs having a common gene pool and characterized appearance/function

Breed Standard – A published document describing the look, movement, and behavior of the perfect specimen of a particular breed

Buff – An off-white to gold coloring

Canine- a term for dog.

Canine Teeth- also known as eye teeth, the largest teeth found in the dog's mouth. They are long, curved teeth on either side of the mouth, top and bottom.

Chronic Disease – refers to a disease that will last indefinitely.

Clip – A method of trimming the coat in some breeds

Coat – The hair covering of a dog; some breeds have two coats, and outer coat and undercoat; also known as a double coat. Examples of breeds with double coats include Shiba Inu, German Shepherd, Siberian Husky, Akita, etc.

Condition – The health of the dog as shown by its skin, coat, behavior, and general appearance

Glossary of Terms

Crate – A container used to house and transport dogs; also called a cage or kennel

Crossbreed (Hybrid) – A dog having a sire and dam of two different breeds; cannot be registered with the AKC

Dam (bitch) – The female parent of a dog;

Dock – To shorten the tail of a dog by surgically removing the end part of the tail.

Double Coat – Having an outer weather-resistant coat and a soft, waterproof coat for warmth; see above.

Drop Ear – An ear in which the tip of the ear folds over and hangs down; not prick or erect

Entropion – A genetic disorder resulting in the upper or lower eyelid turning in

Fancier – A person who is especially interested in a particular breed or dog sport

Fawn – A red-yellow hue of brown

Feathering – A long fringe of hair on the ears, tail, legs, or body of a dog

Groom – To brush, trim, comb or otherwise make a dog's coat neat in appearance

Heel – To command a dog to stay close by its owner's side

Hip Dysplasia – A condition characterized by the abnormal formation of the hip joint

Inbreeding – The breeding of two closely related dogs of one breed

Glossary of Terms

Kennel – A building or enclosure where dogs are kept

Litter – A group of puppies born at one time

Markings – A contrasting color or pattern on a dog's coat

Mask – Dark shading on the dog's foreface

Mate – To breed a dog and a bitch

Neuter – To castrate a male dog or spay a female dog

Pads – The tough, shock-absorbent skin on the bottom of a dog's foot

Parti-Color – A coloration of a dog's coat consisting of two or more definite, well-broken colors; one of the colors must be white

Pedigree – The written record of a dog's genealogy going back three generations or more

Pied – A coloration on a dog consisting of patches of white and another color

Prick Ear – Ear that is carried erect, usually pointed at the tip of the ear

Puppy – A dog under 12 months of age

Purebred – A dog whose sire and dam belong to the same breed and who are of unmixed descent

Saddle – Colored markings in the shape of a saddle over the back; colors may vary

Shedding – The natural process whereby old hair falls off the dog's body as it is replaced by new hair growth.

Glossary of Terms

Sire – The male parent of a dog

Smooth Coat – Short hair that is close-lying

Spay – The surgery to remove a female dog's ovaries, rendering her incapable of breeding

Trim – To groom a dog's coat by plucking or clipping

Undercoat – The soft, short coat typically concealed by a longer outer coat

Vaccine – a shot that is given to a dog to help produce immunity to a specific disease.

Wean – The process through which puppies transition from subsisting on their mother's milk to eating solid food

Whelping – The act of birthing a litter of puppies

Glossary of Terms

Index

A

adaptable	5
adult	43
age	139
allergy	122
appearance	15, 50, 170
award	169

B

barking	108
bath	53
behavior	8
behaviors	60, 95
bitch	172
body	172
breeder	7, 13
breeding	136
breeds	4
brushing	51

C

cage	171
canine	26
care	11
castrate	172
certificate	18

Index

chew 98
choose 6
clippers 58
coat 31, 172
collar 29
coloration 172
colors 172
comb 171
come 75
command 171
commands 66
commercial 48
companion 9
condition 171
crate 63

D

dam 16, 171, 172
diet 45
dig 112
diseases 11, 115
disorder 171
dog-proofing 34
double coat 170
drooling 116

E

ears 59
eating 173
exercise 5
eyes 59

Index

F

face	170
fearfulness	105
feed	35
feeding	42
female	16, 142, 169, 173
food	26
foods	35
foot	172

G

gene	170
genealogy	172
genetic	18, 171
gestation	153
groomer	52
grooming	31, 49
growth	172

H

hair	172
harness	29
health	45
heat	142
height	3
hip	171
history	4
home	26
house	170, 171
housebreaking	60
hunting	4

Index

I

illness	116
ingredients	41
insurance	129
issues	138

K

kennel	17
kibble	36

L

labor	153
leash	29, 100
lie	73
litter	7, 9, 137, 173

M

male	16, 147
markings	172
mate	137
metabolism	38
milk	173
minerals	40

N

nail	57
neuter	128
nutrients	37

Index

O

outer coat	173

P

parent	171
potty training	61
pregnant	148
preparations	134
punishment	84
puppies	158, 173

Q

questions	19

R

raw	40
record	172
registration	133
rescue	12
reward	69

S

senior	44
separation anxiety	79
shelter	12
showing	130
sire	16, 171, 172
sit	72
size	3

Index

skin 50, 118, 172
source 6
spay 128, 172
stay 72
stud 144
supplies 150
surgery 173

T

tail 171
teeth 55, 170
temperament 8, 139
topcoat 50
toys 28
train 4
training 19, 61
treats 28
trimming 57, 170

U

umbilical 65
undercoat 170
urination 117

V

vaccination 125
veterinarian 124
virus 127
vitamins 40

Index

W

weight 3
whelping 150

Index

Photo Credits

Page 3, Leung Cho Pan via Canva.com (Canva Pro License)

https://www.canva.com/photos/MAAvSMj5xCQ-brown-shiba-inu/

Page 6, Bota Sorin via Canva.com (Canva Pro License)

https://www.canva.com/photos/MADZdFN_paE-shiba-inu/

Page 25, Yana_N via Canva.com (Canva Pro License)

https://www.canva.com/photos/MADCAAuo04U-shiba-inu-puppy/

Page 35, Amax Photo via Canva.com (Canva Pro License)

https://www.canva.com/photos/MAEEz5EzAxU-hungry-shiba-inu-dog-is-feeding-at-home-/

Page 49, Изображения пользователя Elena Shvetcova via Canva.com (Canva Pro License)

Photo Credits

https://www.canva.com/photos/MAEb2O3XM08-shiba-inu-dog-in-the-groomer-salon-the-groomer-s-hands-dry-the-wet-wool-with-a-hair-dryer-after-washing-sad-dog-that-doesn-t-like-to-bathe-and-comb/

Page 60, Olga Yastremska's Images via Canva.com (Canva Pro License)

https://www.canva.com/photos/MAEse-1Gg6c-cute-little-shiba-inu-dog-lying-on-doormat-at-home/

Page 115, Thirawatana Phaisalratana via Canva.com (Canva Pro License)

https://www.canva.com/photos/MADC07dqGGc-the-vet-is-feeding-the-puppy-vet-feeding-medicine-with-a-syringe-to-shiba-inu-puppy-veterinarian-give-milk-to-the-puppies-vet-giving-injection-with-syringe-in-dog-/

Page 130, olgaIT via Canva.com (Canva Pro License)

https://www.canva.com/photos/MADAy1BJZpc-japanese-breed-shiba-inu-at-the-dog-show-portrait/

Page 136, fotojagodka via Canva.com (Canva Pro License)

Photo Credits

https://www.canva.com/photos/MADBCdv2DGU-shiba-inu-puppies/

Photo Credits

References

Shiba Inu – Akc.org

https://www.akc.org/dog-breeds/shiba-inu/

Shiba Inu - Dailypaws.com

https://www.dailypaws.com/dogs-puppies/dog-breeds/shiba-inu

Shiba Inu – Dogtime.com

https://dogtime.com/dog-breeds/shiba-inu#/slide/1

6 Authentic Japanese Dog Breeds: Cuteness from Shiba Inu to Akita Inu! - Lisvejapan.com

https://livejapan.com/en/article-a0001799/

The Shiba Inu - Pethealthnetwork.com

https://www.pethealthnetwork.com/dog-health/dog-breeds/shiba-inu

Shiba Inu – Animalhealthcenternh.com

https://animalhealthcenternh.com/client-resources/breed-info/shiba-inu/

Shiba Inu – Petfinder.com

https://www.petfinder.com/dog-breeds/shiba-inu/

References

Shiba Inu- Vetstreet.com

http://www.vetstreet.com/dogs/shiba-inu

All About Shiba Inu - Aspcapetinsurance.com

https://www.aspcapetinsurance.com/resources/shiba-inu/

15 Surprising Facts that Shiba Inu People Need You to Know – Rover.com

https://www.rover.com/blog/surprising-shiba-inu-facts/

The Shiba Inu Care Guide: Personality, History, Food, and More? - Thefarmersdog.com

https://www.thefarmersdog.com/digest/the-shiba-inu-care-guide-personality-history-food-and-more/

Shiba Inu - Be.chewy.com

https://be.chewy.com/dog-breed/shiba-inu/

Shiba Inu – Orvis.com

https://www.orvis.com/shiba-inu.html

Shiba Inu - Springhillvet.com

https://springhillvet.com/client-resources/breed-info/shiba-inu/

Shiba Inu: Dog Breed Profile – Thesprucepets.com

References

https://www.thesprucepets.com/shiba-inu-dog-breed-profile-4775761#where-to-adopt-or-buy-a-shiba-inu

Shiba Inu - Myperkypet.com

https://www.dogbreedslist.info/all-dog-breeds/shiba-inu.html

How To Breed Shiba Inus – Breedingbusiness.com

https://breedingbusiness.com/how-to-breed-shiba-inus/

How to Breed a Shiba Inu - Cuteness.com

https://www.cuteness.com/article/breed-shiba-inu

How to Breed Shiba Inu - Neeness.com

https://neeness.com/how-to-breed-shiba-inu/

All About Shiba Inu Grooming: Bathing & Brushing – Shibatalk.com

https://shibatalk.com/shiba-inu-grooming-bathing-brushing/

Shiba Inu Training Secrets - Shibashake.com

https://shibashake.com/dog/shiba-inu-training-secrets

A Guide To Shiba Inu Training - Canna-pet.com

https://canna-pet.com/guide-shiba-inu-training/

References

Shiba Inu Training Guide: How to Discipline Correctly (Updated 2020) - Norcalshiba.com

https://www.norcalshiba.com/shiba-inu-training/

www.ingramcontent.com/pod-product-compliance
Lightning Source LLC
LaVergne TN
LVHW051831080426
835512LV00018B/2809